Glasgow

THEN AND NOW

Pipe Band Championships
Glasgow Scotland with style
GLASGOW INTERNATIONAL PIPING FESTIVAL
Glasgow Scotland with style
GLASGOW INTERNATIONAL PIPING FESTIVAL
Glasgow

Glasgow

THEN AND NOW

Carol Foreman

BATSFORD

First published in the United Kingdom in 2013 by
Batsford
10 Southcombe Street
London
W14 0RA

An imprint of Anova Books Company Ltd

ISBN: 978-1-84994-075-7

A CIP catalogue record for this book is available from the British Library.

18 17 16 15 14 13
10 9 8 7 6 5 4 3 2 1

Reproduction by Mission Productions Ltd, Hong Kong
Printed by 1010 Printing International Ltd, China

This book can be ordered direct from the publisher at the website: www.anovabooks.com

AUTHOR'S ACKNOWLEDGEMENTS
Thanks are due to David Salmo who asked me to write the book and who, along with his colleague Frank Hopkinson, was always at the other end of an e-mail or phone to answer any queries I might have had. I dedicate the book to my husband John Foreman who had to put up with me vanishing for hours on end, either researching or stuck in front of a computer. Thanks also to photographer Aidan O'Rourke who went to great lengths to try to match up the "now" photographs to the "thens" which was not often easy.

PHOTO CREDITS
The publisher wishes to thank the following for kindly providing photographs for this book:

All 'Then' photographs are courtesy of Carol Foreman, except for the following:
Anova Image Library: 30, 36, 40, 42, 54, 100, 108, 124, 142.
Library of Congress: 1, 6, 46, 62, 72, 106.
Mirrorpix: 20 inset, 24, 74, 82, 130.
Getty Images: 8, 58, 138 main.
Colin Mackie: 84, 125 inset.
Simmons Aerofilms: 126, 140.
Bill Howard: 78.
The Glasgow School of Art Archives and Collections: 94.
Mary Evans Picture Library: 96.
Dennis McCue: 121 inset.

All 'Now' photographs are by Aidan O'Rourke, except for the following:
Carol Foreman: 9, 31, 51, 95, 107 inset, 121 main, 135.
Anova Image Library: 127, 141.
Britannia Panopticon Trust: 35 inset.

Pages 1 and 3 show George Square and the City Chambers, then (Library of Congress) and now (Aidan O'Rourke). See pages 46–47.

Front and back covers show Glasgow Bridge Looking North, then (Library of Congress) and now (Aidan O'Rourke). See pages 72–73.

Introduction

It is appropriate that Glasgow Cathedral should be the first building featured in this book. Glasgow owes its origins to its cathedral, as the site was where Glasgow's patron saint, St Kentigern, popularly called Mungo, founded a religious community and church in 543. The first cathedral built of stone and wood was consecrated on 7 July 1136 by King David I. When it was destroyed by fire in 1172 a rebuilding was begun in 1197 but never finished. Today's building dates from the thirteenth century.

The map of medieval Glasgow is easy to reconstruct. There was an ecclesiastical upper town and a secular lower town. The cathedral sat on high ground on the west bank of the Molendinar Burn, with the Bishop's Palace nearby. Grouped around both was a precinct of manses, one for each of the 32 cathedral canons. The University of Glasgow, founded by papal bull in 1451, was on the east side of High Street, which ran south from the cathedral towards the Clyde. Crossing High Street just below the cathedral was Rottenrow to the west and Drygate to the east, creating Glasgow's first centre. The second, in the lower town where the merchants and artisans lived, was where High Street and its continuation Saltmarket was crossed by Trongate on the west and Gallowgate on the east. This was, and is, Glasgow Cross. After the building of a stone bridge over the river in 1345, Bridgegate and Stockwell Streets were formed. Today, all that remains of medieval Glasgow is the cathedral and one manse, Provand's Lordship, dating from 1471, which formed part of a hospital for the poor dedicated to St Nicholas.

After the Reformation the upper town dwindled in importance, leaving the cathedral isolated from the new commercial centre around Glasgow Cross. It was at the Cross that the Tolbooth – a combination of town hall, courthouse and jail – was erected in 1626. In 1592 the medieval Collegiate Church of St Mary and St Anne in Trongate was reconstructed into the Tron-St Mary's church and the merchants' Guild Hall and hospital was built in Bridgegate in 1665. Today, only the steeples of these buildings remain to remind us of Glasgow's seventeenth-century architecture. That is, apart from a small reminder. The university was rebuilt between 1632 and 1661 and when it was demolished elements of the facade were incorporated into the Pearce Lodge at Gilmorehill.

While imposing new buildings were being erected, the majority of the old wooden thatched houses around the Cross were wiped out in the great fires of 1652 and 1677. Afterwards, all new buildings had to be built of stone, which is when Glasgow's famous Dutch styled tenements with shopping arcades at street level appeared, as shown in the 1865 view of High Street (see page 22).

The eighteenth century saw a tremendous development in trade and wealth and while Glasgow had been violently opposed to the Union in 1707 it gave it the right to trade with the American colonies, once the preserve of the English. The estuary of the Clyde with Glasgow at its head was the most convenient outlet in Britain for trade with America, and thus began the great trade in tobacco on which the city's fortunes were founded.

After 1750, Glasgow expanded rapidly and when a New Town (the Merchant City) was built, the 'Tobacco Lords', or Virginia merchants, built their mansions west of the Cross. Only two remain: No. 42 Miller Street and that build by tobacco merchant William Cunninghame in 1778, now incorporated into the Gallery of Modern Art in Queen Street. To the east, St Andrew's Square was built around St Andrew's Parish Church begun in 1739, while in Charlotte Street David Dale, father of the Scottish cotton industry, built himself a large Palladian villa. George Square was begun in 1782 and St Enoch Square in 1781. Other notable public buildings to appear at this time include the Trades House and Hutchesons' Hall.

By the early nineteenth century, Glasgow had expanded westwards over Blythswood Hill and beyond to Woodlands Hill. The first public building there was the Free Church College designed by Charles Wilson, who also built the classical terraces centred around Park Circus. After the opening of the Botanic Gardens the city moved further west into Kelvinside and Hillhead.

The City Improvement Trust was set up in 1866 to clear slum property and the historic heart of the city, along with the old village of Gorbals, was swept away. This created more problems than it solved. The Trust built too few houses and as displaced people migrated to districts like Cowcaddens even worse slums were created.

By the 1870s, Glasgow was at the peak of its prosperity. It had expanded into the second city of the Empire, inspiring the Victorian builders with the confidence to create a city that came to be recognised as one of the world's finest.

The biggest change in more recent times was the building of the inner ring road that provides easy access to the M8 motorway, but has swept away most of Townhead, Cowcaddens and Anderston.

The last photographs in the book are of the river, which developed from a mere salmon stream into one of the world's finest waterways and harbours. Once famous shipyards lined its banks, but today only the King George V dock remains and steamers no longer depart from the Broomielaw.

To sum up the changes in Glasgow over the centuries: fires swept away the medieval city, the Victorians swept away most of the Georgian city and the twentieth-century city fathers began sweeping away the Victorian buildings until common sense prevailed. This led to Historic Scotland's A, B, and C category listings to protect important buildings.

One difficulty in producing a book such as this is replicating the modern photographs from the same angles as the originals because so much has changed – vantage points have been demolished and new buildings and trees obscure previous ones. But it is these very changes – revealing what was there, what's remained and what's gone – that make the images in this book so fascinating.

GLASGOW CATHEDRAL

The only mainland cathedral in Scotland to survive the Reformation

Left: Dating from the early thirteenth century, Glasgow Cathedral in Castle Street stands over the burial place of St Kentigern, or Mungo, as he is popularly known, Glasgow's patron saint. The first stone cathedral on the site was consecrated in 1136 in the presence of King David I. This was destroyed by fire in 1175 and Bishop Jocelin laid the foundations for a new building consecrated in 1197 but never finished. Today's church was begun by Bishop William de Bondington. At the Reformation, the city's craftsmen persuaded the townspeople to spare the 'idolatrous monument', making it the only mainland cathedral in Scotland to survive. This view, taken from the Necropolis, shows the cathedral around 1870 with the Royal Infirmary and Barony Free Church to the left. Spanning the Molendinar Burn ravine is the Bridge of Sighs (designed by David Hamilton and completed in 1833), so named because of the funeral processions that crossed over it to the Necropolis.

Above: Excluding the profusion of greenery, at first glance this image looks very much like the previous one. However, although the Bridge of Sighs remains, the Molendinar Burn has been culverted and replaced with Wishart Street, named after one of the cathedral's former archbishops. There's still a hospital left of the cathedral, but not the same one. That was replaced by today's much larger Royal Infirmary, which was designed by James Miller and built between 1903 and 1914. Left of the hospital, the Barony Free Church has been demolished and high-rise housing has appeared. The Church of Scotland worships in the cathedral, which is Glasgow's Parish Church as well as a setting for religious, artistic and civic activities. As the building is Crown property it's maintained by Historic Scotland.

GLASGOW, THE NECROPOLIS. 2080 X.
L. S.& P. C

NECROPOLIS

This monumental cemetery was intended to prevent the spread of infectious diseases

Left: This panoramic view of 1900, taken from the cathedral's old burial ground, shows the Necropolis laid out on a hill known as Fir Park owned by the Merchants' House. Set out as a garden cemetery inspired by the Père Lachaise in Paris, it was planned to prevent the spread of infectious diseases including cholera and typhus. Rising up the hill are the 16 sections of the cemetery, each named after letters from the Greek alphabet. Catacombs, vaults and tombs were designed by the city's best architects. Before the formal opening in 1833, the first burial was that of a Jew, Joseph Levy who died of cholera in 1832. Entrance to the cemetery was from Cathedral Square through cast-iron gates installed to provide access to the Bridge of Sighs (see page 7), which carried the carriageway across the Molendinar Burn to the Necropolis. The bridge was described as 'the separation between time and eternity'.

Above: Trees obscure the exact vantage point of the 1900 panorama but this outlook still shows the same monuments on the skyline. The tallest is that of John Knox. Erected in 1825 and intended as the centrepiece of Fir Park, it predated the Necropolis. Inscribed on the base is: 'Chief instrument under God of the Reformation in Scotland.' Overlooking the cathedral, the statue of Knox clutching a bible in his hand had deep religious connotations for the city. To Knox's right is the elaborate Gothic monument (1863) commemorating Duncan MacFarlane, Minister of the Cathedral for over 30 years. Top right, partially covered by trees, is the spectacular mausoleum (1842) of Major Archibald Monteath based on the Knights Templar Church of the Holy Sepulchre in Jerusalem. To appreciate their splendour and gigantic scale, the Greek, Roman, Arabic and Gothic inspired monuments have to be seen close up. There are still regular burials in the cemetery.

BARONY CHURCH

The 'ugliest kirk in all Europe' was demolished in 1886

Left: Possibly taken in the mid 1860s, this photograph shows the cathedral (left) and the Barony Church (right) in Castle Street. The Barony Parish, the most populous in Scotland, was in existence from 1595 until 1985. Its parish church, the Barony, had its beginnings in the Laigh Kirk (Low Church) or crypt of the cathedral. Over the centuries conditions within the crypt became increasingly dark, dirty and damp and by 1798 it was decided to build a new church close to the cathedral. Built by John Robertson to designs by Robert and James Adam it was an ugly mixture of Gothic and Baronial and almost had the appearance of a cement building, the walls being roughcast. Raised in 1799, the church attracted comments both favourable and otherwise on its architectural merits. One of its ministers, Dr Norman Macleod (1812–72) reportedly told Queen Victoria that it was 'the ugliest kirk in all Europe'. Others designated it 'an architectural gem'.

Above: The controversy over the building only ended when time took its toll on it and a new church was required. A site was acquired in Castle Street and the magnificent red sandstone Gothic church designed by J. J. Burnet & J. A. Campbell in 1886 and which incorporated a number of relics and architectural artefacts from the old church, was constructed. Described as possibly the most important Victorian Gothic church in Scotland, it's now the ceremonial Barony Hall of Strathclyde University. When the old Barony was demolished in 1886, the entrance to the Necropolis (right) was realigned to how it is today. Originally the gates and lodge stood further east at the west end of the Bridge of Sighs. There's a statue of the Barony minister Dr Norman Macleod in Cathedral Square Gardens. He served as Moderator of the Church of Scotland as well as chaplain to Queen Victoria. The statue in the foreground is of James White of Overtoun (1812–84), a local employer and co-owner of the J. & J. White Chemical Works.

PROVAND'S LORDSHIP

The oldest house in Glasgow

Left: This 1957 photograph shows Provand's Lordship at the corner of Castle and Macleod Streets surrounded by tenements. It is Glasgow's oldest dwelling house, built by Bishop Andrew Muirhead in 1471 to house the chaplain of the nearby St Nicholas Hospital, an almshouse for aged, poor men. Barely legible on a shield on the south east gable are the Bishop's armorial bearings – three acorns on a bed. The name came about as the house was part of the lands of the Canon of Barlanark whose title was 'Lord of Provan'. While much of the building's exterior is medieval, after the Reformation it came into private hands and in 1670 it was extended. Since then it had many uses including, with a lean-to added, accommodation for the city's hangman. In the 1840s it was a pub and by 1906 it was a sweet shop. In the same year, the Provand's Lordship Society was formed to save the house which was under threat of demolition. Initially the society leased the property but eventually purchased it outright.

Above: In 1978, when major repairs were required, the Provand's Lordship Society offered the property to the City of Glasgow who oversaw its restoration and opened it as a museum in 1983. Inside are three floors, each with three rooms containing furniture dating from the sixteenth, seventeenth and eighteenth century. On the first floor is a reconstruction of the furnished chamber of Cuthbert Simson who lived there as a chaplain at the beginning of the sixteenth century. Behind the house is the St Nicholas Garden created in 1995. As well as a Knot Garden whose shape is based on an ancient Celtic knot design, there's a Physic Garden with herbs and plants used in fifteenth-century medicine. On the walls surrounding the cloister are some of the grotesque Tontine Faces, which were originally the keystones of the Tontine Building at the Cross. As with all of the City of Glasgow's museums, admission to Provand's Lordship is free.

ROYAL INFIRMARY

Where Joseph Lister first experimented with antiseptic surgery

Left: Designed by Robert and James Adam, Glasgow's first Royal Infirmary opened in 1794. It was built on land where the Bishop's Castle had stood. As this view of 1895 shows, the building in Castle Street was typically Adam with giant Venetian windows two-storeys high. There were eight wards each with 17 beds, a circular operating room in the dome and cells in the basement for the temporary confinement of the insane. In 1816, another wing was added and in 1829 a fever block. In 1861, when a surgical block was opened, its death rate rose alarmingly. It had been built on the fringe of the infirmary graveyard and coffins were just below the surface. The situation was remedied and it was in that block in 1865 that Joseph Lister carried out his pioneering antiseptic surgery using carbolic acid to keep wounds and instruments germfree. More pioneering came in 1886, when the Royal set up the world's first hospital X-ray department. The statue in the foreground is of James Lumsden (1778–1856), Lord Provost of Glasgow and treasurer of the Royal Infirmary for 19 years.

Above: In 1897 it was decided that a modern building should replace the hospital, including the Adam front block. James Miller's design was chosen despite concerns that its proposed size would dwarf the cathedral. Part of the new hospital opened in 1909 and in 1911 the Adam block was demolished and replaced with Miller's classical building, shown here partially obscured with trees and scaffolding. King George V opened the Queen Victoria Jubilee Block in 1914 and incorporated in it is the foundation stone of the old infirmary. Despite pleas and objections to preserve it, in 1924 it was decided to pull down the famous Lister Ward. A reconstruction of it can be seen in the Wellcome Medical Museum in London and the fireplace and a table was gifted to the Royal Faculty of Physicians and Surgeons of Glasgow in St Vincent Street. Added between 1971 and 1982 to the already enormous bulk of the hospital was the huge Queen Elizabeth Block.

THE GLASGOW
HIPPODROME
AND
VARIETY
THEATRE
adjoining ZOO
NEW CITY ROAD
The Best Place
OF AMUSEMENT
IN THE CITY

LADYWELL STREET / TENNENT'S WELLPARK BREWERY

Glasgow's most ancient street was named after the nearby Well of Our Lady

Left: The last thatched house in Glasgow, seen here in the early 1890s, was in Ladywell Street, one of the city's most ancient paths having originally been the main route from the south-east up to the cathedral. The name came from the nearby Lady Well (Well of Our Lady). As can be seen, the house was much older than the adjoining buildings. It had two small attics and an outside stair with a jawbox (a sink used by all the tenants) that led up to the door of the middle flat. At one time the building was the residence of William Calcraft (1800–79), the public hangman who was remembered as being accompanied by two huge mastiffs. In consequence, the slope was known locally as 'hangman's brae'. On the east side of the street was Glasgow's earliest 'ragged school', where the Bible and Dr Johnson's *Dictionary of the English Language* were the main books used for instruction.

Above: The Lady Well was an artesian spring noted on early city maps. Lying just outside the city wall it was erroneously believed to have been sunk for use of commoners denied access to the nearby Priest's Well. When the Necropolis opened in 1833, a scare arose, as it was thought that the source of the spring had been tainted owing to its proximity to the graves. In deference to this it was closed but the site was marked by a niche built into the wall containing an iron urn (see inset). An inscription on the lintel stone states that it was restored in 1836 and rebuilt it 1874 by the Merchants' House. A plaque commemorates Tennent Caledonian Breweries' restoration in 1983. Nowadays all that remains of Ladywell Street has been swallowed up by Tennent's Wellpark Brewery. The scaffolded spire of the cathedral can be seen in the distance.

R.&J.TEMPLETON
OIL & COLOUR STO

BELL O' THE BRAE

The crown of this hill was the site of a legendary battle

Left: Pictured here around 1900 is the Bell o' the Brae at the intersection of the High Street with George and Duke Streets. The term applied to the highest part of the slope of a hill, 'bel' signifying a prominence. The dangerously steep hill of medieval times was first lowered in 1783, removing seventeenth-century thatched cottages that were replaced by the buildings in the view. The Bell o' the Brae was the location of a battle around 1300 between Sir William Wallace and the English garrisoned in the Bishop's Castle beside the cathedral. When Wallace's men attacked the English they were chased down the High Street. But, as planned, the Scots turned to fight and another Scottish force, led by Wallace's uncle, Auchinleck, attacked from the rear. Hemmed in, the English were defeated. Apocryphal or not, most histories of Glasgow include it.

Above: Nothing is recognisable from the previous view. Everything was demolished under the auspices of the pioneering City Improvement Act of 1866, which set up a trust to redevelop the slum localities of Trongate, Saltmarket, Gallowgate and the High Street. Included were parts of Calton and the Gorbals. The eighteenth-century buildings were replaced by 1905 with an impressive broad curve of four-storey, red sandstone City Improvement Trust tenements with shops below. With big chimneystacks, attic-level oriels, crow-stepped gables and panels carved with the city's arms, the competition-winning design in 1899 by Burnet, Boston and Carruthers was an Arts and Crafts interpretation of a Scottish seventeenth-century tenement. Described as 'model homes' for working people, the B-listed buildings are considered among the best built by the City Improvement Trust.

OLD COLLEGE (UNIVERSITY OF GLASGOW) / HIGH STREET STATION

Once the finest group of seventeenth-century buildings in Scotland

Left: This 1860s photograph shows the University of Glasgow, or the Old College as it was then called. Founded by papal bull in 1451, it met in various places until it was endowed with land in the High Street. Building began in 1632 but was interrupted by the Civil War and it was not until 1661 that the complex was completed. Shown here is the Scottish Jacobean facade with a cab waiting at the heavily ornamented college gateway, whose massive oak nail-studded doors were closed at night. Behind the frontage were two quadrangles, the inner having a 43m (140ft) Dutch-style steeple topped with a gilded cock on the spear. There was no clock until 1686. The outer quadrangle held the Lion and Unicorn Staircase of 1690 (shown inset). To the south of the complex was the college church of 1699. Behind the buildings were seven acres of pleasure grounds reaching down to the Molendinar Burn.

Above: When the previous photograph was taken, the college was surrounded by some of the city's worst slums. Two streets in particular, the Havannah and the New Vennel were the filthiest and most disease-ridden. A decision was made to build a new university at Gilmorehill and the college and land was sold to the Glasgow Union Railway Company in 1863. Despite public outcry, the college was demolished in 1870 – a blunder that resulted in Scotland losing its finest group of seventeenth-century buildings. Some common sense did prevail, however. The Lion and Unicorn Staircase was transferred to Gilmorehill along with part of the facade, now incorporated into Pearce Lodge (see page 107). College Goods Station was built on the site. The station closed in 1958 and today a multi-storey car park and High Street Station occupy the site, along with the beginnings of the Collegelands residential and commercial development.

M'ILVENNY'S LODGINGS
LODGINGS
WORKING
MEN &
TRAVELLERS
GLASGOW ABS
29
HARDWARE

HIGH STREET

These 'squalid and repulsive' piazzas were demolished under the City Improvement Act

Left: These two tenements on the west side of High Street were the last of Glasgow's famous arcaded buildings. The piazza, or shopping arcade, at one time continued along the four principal streets – High Street, Trongate, Saltmarket and Gallowgate. Shown here around 1865, the tenements dated from the early seventeenth century. They were built of stone after devastating fires in 1652 and 1677 destroyed most of the old timber buildings in the area. The council ordained that there would be no more inflammable timber projections and that all new buildings should be of stone. Their design was reminiscent of Dutch architecture with the gable on the front. Lack of building space necessitated vertical rather than horizontal building. The arches were blocked up after the 1800 Glasgow Police Act described them as 'receptacles for thieves, pickpockets and idle and disorderly persons'.

Above: By 1853 the High Street and its stinking vennels, according to writer Hugh MacDonald, had become 'squalid and repulsive and where sin and misery are to be seen in loathsome union'. It was notorious for its overcrowding and it was no surprise therefore that when the City Improvement Act of 1866 was passed in order to open and rebuild the densely inhabited areas of the city centre that the High Street was high on the list for redevelopment. As the previous view shows, the two tenements, the last relics of the famous piazzas admired by generations of travellers, had degenerated into cheap lodging houses. Before their demolition in the mid 1870s they were photographed and measured for architectural archiving. Their replacement was this City Improvement Trust range of towering, red sandstone warehouses.

TOLBOOTH STEEPLE

One of only three crown spires in Scotland

Left: The Tolbooth Steeple was originally part of the municipal building built at Glasgow Cross in 1626. Its seven storeys gave access to the tolbooth and the prison. The crown spire was one of the only three such spires in Scotland, the other two being St Giles' Cathedral in Edinburgh and King's College in Aberdeen. Originally the steeple had 28 bells, which were replaced in 1881 by 16 small bells and one large one. When the civic centre moved to Saltmarket in 1817 the tolbooth was rebuilt and what we see in this image of around 1915 is its very similar replacement. It had been touch and go as to whether the steeple would be retained and the city fathers only agreed by a majority of 15 votes to nine to keep it. Left is the entrance to Glasgow Cross Railway Station that opened in 1895.

Right: The tolbooth, latterly occupied by John A. Bowman, 'Auctioneer and Valuater', was demolished in 1921 after it was destroyed by fire. The steeple was once again under threat of demolition, this time to ease the flow of traffic into High Street. Fortunately it got another stay of execution and instead the road was widened, leaving it marooned on an island. By 1932, set back on the building line, the tolbooth had been replaced by the first quadrant of a classical competition-winning scheme to enclose the cross with a vast semi-circle of steel-framed, stone-clad mercantile premises. As we can see, the east quadrant wasn't built and today a modern housing block takes its place. The station closed in 1964 and the only evidence of its existence is the decorative ventilation grilles on the traffic island. There are often rumours of it reopening.

TONTINE HOTEL
ALL WORKING MEN'S CLUB

TONTINE HOTEL

Built at the height of Glasgow's successful American tobacco trade

Left: The Tontine Hotel at Glasgow Cross, pictured here around 1865, was intended as a new town hall to replace the antiquated one in the Tolbooth Steeple. Built in two sections, the first was completed in 1740. The lower storey formed a broad piazza with five arches whose keystones were ornamented with grotesque stone faces sculpted by Mungo Naismith. The western half was added in 1760. In 1781 the Tontine Society acquired the town hall, which was reconstructed as a Coffee Room and Hotel. The Coffee Room, or Exchange as it became, was the commercial centre of Glasgow and for a yearly subscription members had access to most British and European newspapers. The hotel was often referred to as the 'Tontine Hottle' as it was the first of its kind in Glasgow and the citizens were unused to the word 'hotel'. By the 1860s it had become a Working Men's Club. The statue commemorates William of Orange, King Billy to Glaswegians.

Above: In 1867 the Improvement Trustees bought the building and converted it into a shop, which drapers Moore Taggart occupied until 1911 when it was seriously damaged by fire and had to be demolished. The red sandstone warehouse seen here replaced Glasgow's finest eighteenth-century building, which had once expressed the new-found civic pride that the city was beginning to feel with its highly successful American tobacco trade. The name Tontine lives on in the lane alongside the building and the salvaged keystones of the arches. The famous Tontine Heads can now be seen in the St Nicholas Garden behind Provand's Lordship. The controversial William of Orange statue that stood in the Trongate for 189 years is now in Cathedral Square. It's known as the statue with the moving tail. When the tail got damaged it was repaired with a ball-and-socket arrangement which meant that every time the wind blew the tail could be seen to move.

ST ANDREW'S PARISH CHURCH

The A-listed building is now a centre for Scottish music

Left: The A-listed St Andrew's Parish Church in St Andrew's Square near Glasgow Cross, is regarded as one of the UK's top six classical churches. It was constructed in 1739 to the designs of Allan Dreghorn and built by master mason Mungo Naismith. Reputed to resemble St Martin in the Fields in London, it was the first Prestbyterian church built after the Reformation. This 1920s view shows the church from the south east. The front (see inset opposite) has six tall Corinthian columns supporting a pediment bearing Glasgow's coat of arms, above which is a clock tower with an octagonal bell chamber. Later, the church was enclosed by a square which became the fashionable address of the wealthiest merchants before the city expanded westwards. In 1785 Glaswegians gathered to watch Vincenzo Lunardi take off from behind the church in a hot-air balloon on a flight taking him south-east to Hamilton and Lanark before landing in Hawick.

Right: After almost 240 years of continuous service as a church, the last service was held in June 1993. The building was considered to be at risk and the church's dwindling congregation requested that ownership be transferred to the Glasgow Preservation Trust. The announcement that the Trust was to proceed with the restoration of the church prompted the redevelopment of St Andrew's Square, whose once-fine residences had become warehouses and workshops. The church restoration involved the creation of a basement, the removal of Victorian additions, and the reinstating of the magnificent baroque interior, complete with ornate gilded plaster ceiling and Corinthian columned nave. The building officially opened on 30 November 2000 – St Andrew's Day – as a Centre for Traditional Scottish Music, Song and Dance.

FUNERAL
OFFICE
GLASGOW.
GLASGOW CROSS PAWNBROKING
STAMPING
FOR
W. COCHRANE

SALTMARKET

Once the most fashionable address in Glasgow

Left: This c. 1885 view of Saltmarket from London Street (now London Road) shows an eighteenth-century Dutch gabled building alongside a plainer tenement. The street used to be called Waulkergate – the way to the colony of fullers or cloth waulkers who lived in a cluster of houses near the river. It changed to Saltmarket in 1650 when the market that sold salt for the curing of salmon was sited there. The thoroughfare, which linked Glasgow Cross to the head of the Briggait (Bridgegate), was once the city's most fashionable address. James IV stayed there, as did Oliver Cromwell when he visited the city in 1650. The arrival of slaughterhouses, bleachfields and the Judiciary Courts brought its desirability as a residential area to an end. In the early part of the nineteenth century it was where the Glasgow Fair was held. Most of medieval Saltmarket was destroyed in the fires of 1652 and 1677.

Above: When the City Improvement Trust rebuilt Saltmarket in the 1890s the building line was moved southwards so that London Road bypassed it, meaning that the buildings in the previous view would today be halfway across London Road at the intersection of Saltmarket and Trongate pictured here. The new buildings included apartment houses above a row of shops – the city's first municipal housing for the artisan classes. Their crow-stepped gables and chimneys acknowledged the style of the seventeenth-century buildings that were swept away to make way for them. John Carrick, the City Architect who prepared the plans for the experimental range of tenements, incorporated some of his own favourite ideas, like the two toilets on each landing – one for each sex. At the corner of Saltmarket and Bridgegate, the Ship Bank pub has window glass etched with a depiction of the eighteenth-century Ship Bank that once stood at the junction.

PERCY'S
426

TRONGATE

This busy thoroughfare once led to the Tron – a public weighing beam

Left: A thronging Trongate facing east, pictured here in the late 1880s. The name originated from the Tron – the public weighing beam – that this street once led to. Merchandise brought into the town was subject to tolls and customs collected by the Tolbooth official after they had been weighed at the Tron in Glasgow Cross. Middle left is the Tolbooth Steeple, but dominating the view is the Tron Church steeple. This was added to the Collegiate Church of St Mary and St Anne, founded in 1485 and reconstructed as the Tron-St Mary's Kirk in 1592, the year the tower was begun. The stone spire was added in 1636. In 1793, when the church was burnt down by the Hell Fire Club, the steeple survived and in 1794 a new church designed by James Adam was built behind it. The pedestrian arches were cut through the tower in 1855.

Above: The Tron Church continued as a place of worship until 1946. It then fell into disrepair until the Glasgow Theatre Club, formed in 1979, leased it and in 1981 established the Tron Theatre there. Performances took place in the Victorian Bar, until the opening of the main auditorium in 1982. After being awarded £5 million for an extensive redevelopment project, the fully refurbished theatre reopened in 1999 and in 2006 celebrated 25 years of performances. At first glance this image looks as though little has changed architecturally. However, the building on the right-hand corner has been replaced by a City Improvement Trust tenement. The low building on the left has also been replaced and a domed red sandstone range of offices now partially obscures the Tolbooth Steeple. Beyond the steeple is a modern residential development.

BRITANNIA MUSIC HALL

One of the world's oldest surviving music halls

Left: The Britannia Music Hall in Trongate is shown here c. 1892. Situated on the first and second floors of a warehouse built in 1857, it started life in 1872 as Campbell's Music Salon, an unlicensed music hall. By 1859 it was owned by John Brand and renamed the Britannia. Its entrance was sandwiched between two shop fronts and marked only by two gas lanterns. The auditorium had a single wooden balcony with bench seating throughout. The Britannia avoided the sale of alcohol and Brand was said to run it along temperance lines. Police reports detailing the debauchery of similar establishments described the Britannia as a model of good management and decorum. At the 'Brit' unfavourable acts had rotten fruit and eggs hurled at them. A regular feature was the Friday amateur night when any aspiring artiste who didn't please was yanked off stage by the manager using a long pole with a hook on the end.

Right: By the end of the 1890s Glasgow had more theatres per head of population than any other city in the country and the Britannia was the Grand Old Lady where stars such as Marie Lloyd and Vesta Tilley appeared. When Albert Hubner took over the management in 1892 he showed silent films as an added attraction, renaming the building Hubner's Cinematograph. New built theatres halted the Brit's popularity and it closed in 1903. In 1906 Yorkshire-born businessman Albert Edward Pickard leased it. As he already owned the adjacent waxworks he named his complex the Panopticon, 'a place where you can see everything' he said. Stan Laurel made his debut there. The Panopticon closed in 1938 and lay hidden by a false ceiling until the 1990s. Today, the trust conserving it performs traditional shows in the auditorium shown inset. While funding enabled restoration work on the exterior of the A-listed building, the theatre itself needs much work.

WILSON STREE

COUNTY BUILDINGS AND COURTHOUSE

Now home to the Scottish Youth Theatre

Left: Shown here around 1890 is the massive former County Buildings and Courthouse in Wilson Street that fills a whole block of the Merchant City. In 1841 architects William Clarke and George Bell won a competition to design a building to accommodate the Town Council, a County Sheriff Court and the Merchants' House. Opened in 1844, the council offices and court faced south to Wilson Street. Dominating the facade was a Greek Ionic portico standing above a classical frieze containing representations of the work of the justice system. The Merchants' House was placed at the north end of the site. Topped by a colonnade of Corinthian columns, its entrance faced west to Garthland Street (now Garth Street). The plan enabled each section of the building to have a separate identity. When the Merchants' House moved out in 1870, the council added an extension to the north. By 1888 the council had moved to George Square leaving the whole building as a courthouse.

Above: Over the decades the Sheriff Courthouse's demand outstripped available accommodation and in 1932 it was decided that a new building was necessary. This was not achieved until 1986 when the new Sheriff Court of Glasgow and Strathkelvin in the Gorbals opened. No one seemed to know what to do with the enormous old building and it lay empty and neglected. One idea was to turn it into a Museum of Costume. Another was for it to be converted into an international hotel. Eventually, after a renovation, the facade was retained around a new interior structure which has a mixed residential and commercial use. The addition of a modern glazed storey now sits uncomfortably on top of this otherwise dignified classical building. The Scottish Youth Theatre has its headquarters in the building and there are five individual rehearsal spaces, a dance studio, a studio theatre, a Board Room and a private and secure courtyard offering the opportunity to be 'outside, inside'.

RAMSHORN CHURCH

Scotland's first example of Neo-Gothic Revival

Left: This photograph of the Ramshorn Church in Ingram Street was taken in 1975. Its proper name is St David's but because it was built on the Ramshorn lands it has always been known by that name, as was its predecessor of 1720 that was demolished to form Ingram Street. Built in 1824, the church, Scotland's first example of the Neo-Gothic Revival, was the work of Birmingham architect Thomas Rickman. James Cleland, Glasgow's Town Superintendent of Public Works, modified the design and was responsible for the neck-breaking stair and the crypt where many of Glasgow's mercantile princes are buried. The church contains an outstanding collection of stained glass said to be 'arguably the finest Victorian stained glass in Scotland'. Installed during refurbishment in 1886, most of it was produced in Glasgow. That the windows have survived is amazing as they have been removed three times in their life.

Right: As the congregation had dwindled, the Church of Scotland sold the church to the University of Strathclyde in 1982. Ten years later the university converted it into a public theatre. It became home to Strathclyde Theatre Group and was also used by touring companies. The university has a much older connection with the church in that its founder Professor John Anderson worshipped there in the eighteenth century and is buried in the crypt. The Ramshorn can be visited during Doors Open Day, when hundreds of interesting buildings are opened free to the public. The scheme was first introduced to the UK by Glasgow Preservation Trust as part of the 1990 Glasgow City of Culture celebrations. A recently restored Ramshorn Church is currently being used for teaching and the university is restoring the parts of the graveyard that have fallen into disrepair.

HUTCHESONS' HALL

This A-listed building is currently closed to the public

Left: Hutchesons' Hall in Ingram Street, shown here in the 1950s, is one of the most elegant buildings in the city centre. It was built in 1802–05 as a replacement for the hall lost when the seventeenth-century Hutchesons' Hospital in the Trongate was demolished. Founded in 1639 by philanthropic brothers George and Thomas Hutcheson, it provided shelter for several poor, aged tradesmen and a school for 12 boys, those named Hutcheson being given preference. This was the forerunner of Hutchesons' Grammar School. Architect David Hamilton deliberately designed the new hall to look older so that it would retain something of the atmosphere of the original. Recessed behind Corinthian columns, the principal storey is flanked by niches holding statues of George and Thomas Hutcheson carved in 1649. They came from the old hospital and are believed to be the only seventeenth-century figures left in Glasgow. The unusual clock tower is a well-known landmark.

Right: Hutchesons' Hall was never again used as a hospital. Instead, it became a meeting place for the patrons of the charity, who were given assistance by way of pensions rather than by shelter after the destruction of the Trongate building. The frieze is inscribed: 'Founded by George and Thomas Hutcheson of Lambhill 1639 & 1641 – rebuilt 1805.' While nothing changed on the outside, a remodelling of the interior in 1876 by John Baird II turned the first floor hall into one of the finest rooms in Glasgow. To create it, the second floor schoolroom was used by Hutchesons' Grammar School until the remodelling was removed. This allowed for a dramatic double-height hall with detailed plasterwork and stained glass depicting portraits of the founders and the old hospital. When the National Trust took over the property the Grand Hall was hung with portraits of Glasgow worthies and made available for conferences and functions. The building is currently closed to the public.

NO ENTRY
FOR
HANDCARTS
HORSEDRAWN
AND
SLOW MOVING
VEHICLES
UNLESS REQUIRING ACCESS
TO PREMISES NOT
OTHERWISE ACCESSIBLE
CIGARETTES

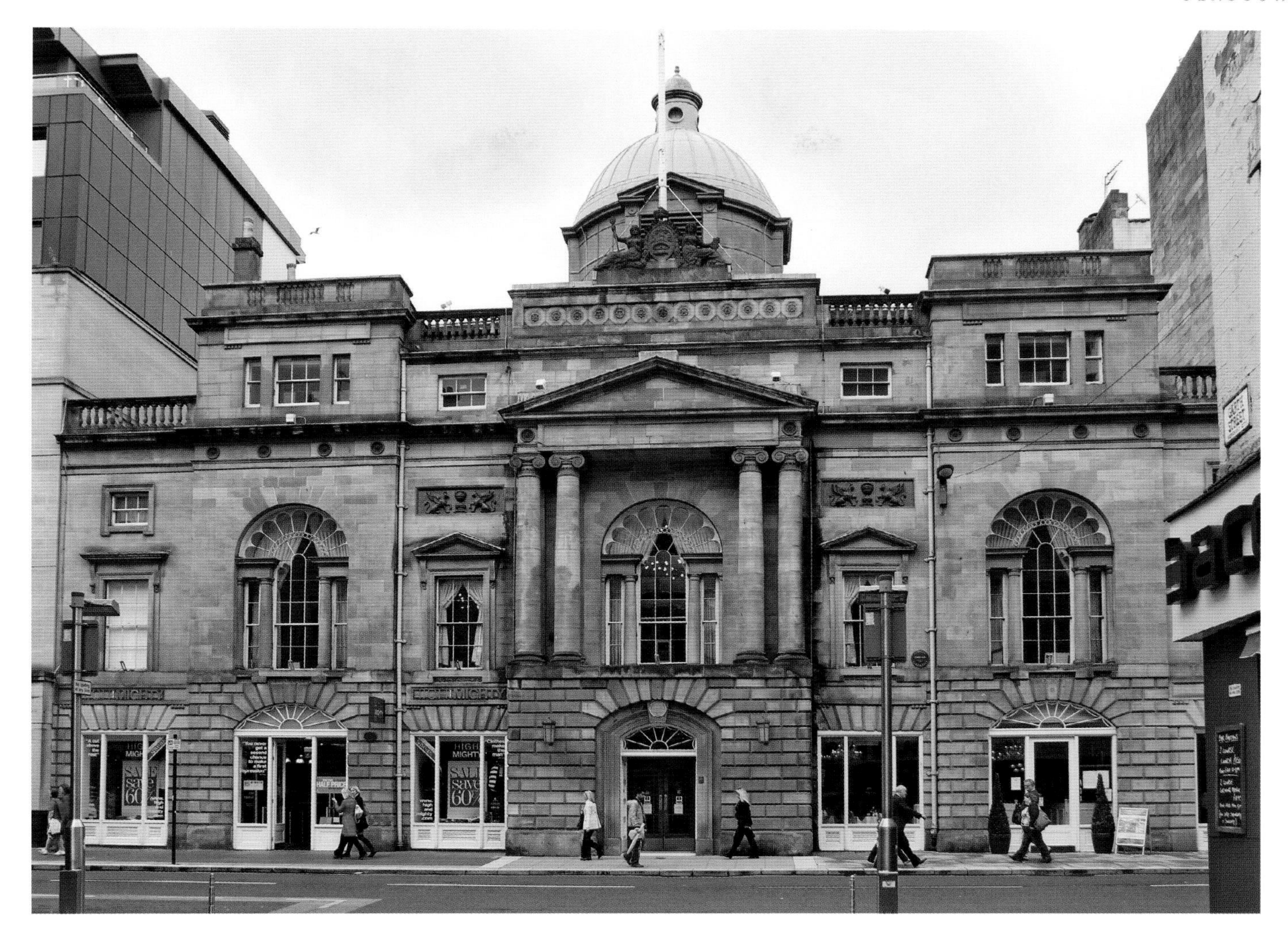

TRADES HOUSE

Glasgow's 14 trade crafts have been served by the Trades House since 1605

Left: In 1605 Glasgow's fourteen trade crafts federated as the Trades House led by a Deacon Convenor. Besides its trade and burgh activities, it provided hospitals (almshouses) for the sick, pensions for the elderly and succour for the needy. Today it meets in the Trades Hall, the oldest secular building in the city used for its original purpose. Located in Glassford Street, it's Glasgow's only surviving Robert Adam building. Completed in 1794 and pictured here in the early 1950s, it is Palladian in style with a raised Ionic portico and a well-proportioned dome. Over its lifetime it has been altered and added to, the outer bays being nineteenth-century additions. In 1808 the incorporations set up a school for boys and girls. The Trades House paid the schoolmaster's salary and the school met in the Trades Hall. It was discontinued when the Education Act of 1872 made public education compulsory. By then, over 100 children had been taught the three Rs.

Above: Externally the building is unchanged but in 1954, due to traffic vibration, the plaster ceiling in the Banqueting Hall became unsafe and had to be taken down. The new ceiling was made of fire-proofed wood and the dome, displaying the crests of the fourteen crafts, was set into it. Below the ceiling there's a nineteenth-century Belgian silk frieze depicting the work of the trades and the type of equipment each used. The magnificent chandeliers came from the old Grosvenor Restaurant in Gordon Street. During refurbishment in 2001 the shell of the old schoolroom, complete with rows of wooden benches, was discovered hidden in the top floor under the parapet. The Trades House continues to serve the needs of the fourteen crafts, which includes Hammermen, Bonnetmakers and Glovers. Along with Glasgow Cathedral, the Trades House is the most significant surviving link with the city's past and keeps alive many of Glasgow's earliest traditions.

42 MILLER STREET

The last of the grand tobacco merchants' houses

Left: The oldest house in the Merchant City photographed in 1977. Number 42 Miller Street – the last of the so-called Virginia tobacco merchants' houses to survive in entirety – looks out of place among its tall neighbours. Designed in 1775 by John Craig in Palladian style it was built on land feued from the garden of John Miller, whom the street is named after. Miller influenced the design by regulating, among other stipulations, that there would be no gables, or corbie-stepped chimneys facing the street. Also, there was to be no brewing, tanning of leather, making candles or soap, or any other business that could be 'nauseous' or 'hurtful' to the inhabitants of the street. The first resident was the leading Glasgow merchant family of Robert Findlay. From 1836 until 1866 the City and Suburban Gas Company used it as offices. Thereafter a succession of businesses occupied it.

Right: From 1989, the building lay derelict and slowly decaying, but in 1992 it was offered to the Glasgow Building Preservation Trust for £1. Restoration began in October 1994 and was completed the following October when the Preservation Trust became its first new occupant. Externally, the restoration attempted to reinstate exactly the original appearance of the building. The ugly mansard was removed, along with the single-pane sash Victorian windows that were replaced with crown glass Georgian style ones. Internally, new plasterwork and joinery were reproduced to original profiles and the original room layout was recreated. Today No. 42 is an A-listed building of 'national importance' and its restoration received a Heritage Award from Historic Scotland. The Scottish Civic Trust acquired the building in 1997 and to mark the acquisition the Prince of Wales, Patron of the Trust, opened it on 28 January 1998 by unveiling a commemorative plaque.

GEORGE SQUARE AND THE CITY CHAMBERS

The City Chambers demonstrated the opulence of Glasgow in its Victorian heyday

Left: This elevated 1890 view shows George Square and the City Chambers. The square was named after King George III and although laid out in 1781 not much more was done other than mark its boundary. It was described as 'a hollow filled with green water and a favourite spot for drowning cats and dogs'. Occupying the east side is the City Chambers, which its architect John Young styled as 'a free and dignified treatment of the Italian Renaissance'. It shows more clearly than any other building in the city the opulence of Glasgow in its Victorian heyday. Queen Victoria performed the inauguration ceremony in 1888. It's one of only two buildings in Europe to have three floors dressed in marble. The other's the Vatican. Of the twelve statues in the square, the tallest is that of Sir Walter Scott. The equestrian bronze in front of the City Chambers commemorates Prince Albert. Right is the A-listed Italianate Post Office of 1875.

Above: Although the panorama is relatively unchanged, the colour of the asphalt covering the square has earned it the nickname of Red Square. When this was done in the 1970s there was a public outcry. The statue of Prince Albert has been moved to the opposite end of the square alongside that of Queen Victoria. In its place is the Cenotaph in remembrance of the 18,000 Glasgow men who died during the First World War. Designed by Sir J. J. Burnet, the truncated obelisk is flanked with sculptures of lions by Ernest Gillick. Lying horizontally between the lions is a sculptured wreath and a palm frond together with the single word *Pax* (Peace). On the face is a gilded metal cross in the form of a sword. Earl Haig unveiled the monument in 1924. Beyond the City Chambers there's now a multi-storey building and to the right the former Post Office is now an exclusive residential development. The temporary marquees and seating shown here were set up for the 2012 World Pipe Band Championship.

BANQUETING HALL, CITY CHAMBERS

A sumptuous room with murals depicting the city's history and progress

Left: Magnificent though the exterior of the City Chambers is, the true expression of Victorian opulence comes from within. The entrance hall or Loggia, as architect John Young called it, is overwhelmingly sumptuous. There are two breathtaking staircases. The one leading to the Banqueting Hall is solid veined carrara marble and the largest three-storey marble staircase in Europe. Despite competition from the rest of the building, the vast coffered double-height, barrel-vaulted Banqueting Hall is the Chambers' *pièce de résistance*. Clearly showing the influence of the French buildings visited by the Council's advisory committee, it holds its own against anything Venice can offer. The splendid chandeliers or 'electroliers', have their own story to tell as in 1885 the council decided that the hall should have electric lighting, a cutting-edge innovation then. This photograph from 1888 shows the undecorated Banqueting Hall when the building had just been completed.

Above: Under the advice and supervision of architect William Leiper, the Banqueting Hall was decorated with huge murals emblematic of the city's history and progress. Painted in 1899 by the 'Glasgow Boys' collective, they were then the most modern work the city could offer. The lunette over the platform has George Henry's mural representing King William the Lion granting a charter in 1175, making Glasgow a Burgh of Barony with the right to hold a weekly market. To the right, on the wall nearest the stage, is Alexander Roche's *Legendary Glasgow* depicting an incident in one of the legendary stories to which the design of Glasgow's city crest owes its origin. The centre mural painted by Edward Walton portrays Glasgow Fair as it was about the end of the fifteenth century, when it was farming orientated with horse and cattle markets. Further right, but not in view, is Sir John Lavery's *Modern Glasgow* representing local industry.

ICTORIA GALLERY.
PHOTOGRAPHERS.
MERCHANTS BUILDINGS. GLASGOW. 2793. G.W.W.

WEST SIDE OF GEORGE SQUARE

This Italianate range combines the work of J. T. Rochead, James Sellers and John Burnet

Left: The Italianate range of the west side of George Square was built in stages. In this c. 1890 photograph, the Bank of Scotland by J. T. Rochead (1869) is on the left with an addition by James Sellars (1874) in the middle and the Merchants' House by John Burnet (1877) on the right. Like the Trades House, the Merchants' House was created in 1605. Led by a Dean of Guild, the original Merchants' Hall in Bridgegate was a meeting place for the merchants and a hospital (almshouse) for members who had fallen on hard times. By the time the hall was rebuilt in 1650 most of the charity was being expended in pensions. When it was sold there was a proviso that its steeple, which had become a local landmark, had to be retained. After a stay in Hutcheson Street, the Merchants' House moved into George Square where the tower bore a model ship atop a globe replicating that on the original steeple.

Above: Rochead's Bank of Scotland set the style for the whole range. Sellers followed his design for the middle section with the addition of an attic storey. Burnet's wing echoed Rochead's until he added the tower and dome to the corner. Without it the whole range formed a single symmetrical palace design with a higher central section. Symmetry was further spoiled in 1909 with the addition of two storeys. Designed by Burnet's son, these were skilfully concealed behind giant columns. The storey above the main entrance in 7 West George Street has a sculpture featuring a pair of caryatids on either side of a ship atop a globe. The engraved phrase *Toites reduntis oedem* (so often returning to the same place) is the Merchants' House emblem. Headquartered in the building is the Glasgow Chamber of Commerce, the oldest chamber in the English-speaking world with a continuous existence.

TH BRITISH RAILWAY
EN STREET STATION
TO THE PARCEL OFFICE
PARCELS
OFFICE
TAY
BRIDGE
ROUTE
EDINBURGH
YORK, HULL
QUEEN STREET STATION
NORTH BRITISH RAILWAY
CAB OFFICE
TH BRITISH RAILWAY
JEYES
FLUID
Glasgow.
Queen Street. Station.

QUEEN STREET STATION

Glasgow's oldest surviving railway station

Left: Queen Street Station opened in 1842 as the Glasgow terminus of the Edinburgh & Glasgow Railway. The tunnel between Queen Street and Cowlairs was the greatest engineering feat ever attempted in Scotland. However, a major obstacle was the Cowlairs Incline, a steep slope with a gradient of 1 in 46 which required trains to be hauled from the station by means of a steam-driven winding cable. Nothing was left of the original station when it was rebuilt and expanded by the North British Railway in 1878–88, which is when the iron-arched glass roof was erected and electric lighting was introduced. Opened in 1886, the Low Level station had to be excavated without disturbing the main line traffic above. This image shows the station around 1910 with rows of horse-drawn vans lined up outside the goods office.

Above: Queen Street Station is the third busiest in Scotland. The station serves northern and eastern Scotland with lines running to destinations such as Perth, Aberdeen and Inverness. It runs a shuttle service to Edinburgh every fifteen minutes, the journey taking approximately forty-five minutes. Low Level serves the outskirts of the city to the east and west. The stretch of this line between High Street, Queen Street and Charing Cross was built before the Glasgow Subway (1896), making it the oldest underground railway in the city. When Buchanan Street Station closed in 1966 its services were transferred to Queen Street causing difficulties with longer trains as the station is in a confined position. The problem of the Cowlairs Incline was solved with the introduction of diesel trains that could handle it independently. Today the station's outstanding feature, the iron and glass arched roof, is obscured by this 1969 building.

ROYAL EXCHANGE GLASGOW

ROYAL EXCHANGE SQUARE

Once the site of an eighteenth-century tobacco trader's house

Left: Royal Exchange Square is shown here c. 1920. Developed from 1827 onwards, nothing like it exists in Europe. It is built around a notable building whose beginnings go back to 1778, when William Cunninghame built a fine Tobacco Lord's house in a large garden. When the Royal Bank bought it in 1817, it commissioned Archibald Elliot II to prepare plans for a new bank to the rear and terraces of shops and business chambers to the north and south. In 1827, the mansion and remaining land was sold for conversion into a Royal Exchange. Architect David Hamilton added the massive Corinthian columned portico to the front, above which rose a cupola and clock tower. The Exchange's hall, with its magnificent barrel-vaulted ceiling, was added at the back leaving the house sandwiched in between, as this view shows. Added in 1880, the mansard housed Glasgow's first telephone exchange. The equestrian statue by Baron Carlo Marochetti (1844) commemorates the Duke of Wellington.

Above: In 1949 Glasgow Corporation purchased the Exchange to accommodate Stirling's Library and the Commercial Library, which opened in 1954. Later, the council converted the building into the Gallery of Modern Art (GOMA), which opened in 1996. The modernistic treatment of the city's coat of arms on the pediment caused controversy as it was at odds with the building's classical architecture. The four floors of galleries exhibit paintings and sculptures from around the world including those of David Hockney and Andy Warhol. In 2002 the library moved back into the basement where it has a café, free internet access and book-lending facilities. The statue of the Duke of Wellington has become iconic for the traffic cones that are constantly replaced on its head. For years, every time cones appeared they were removed. Now they are left alone and the statue is mentioned in guide books as a tourist attraction. Inset is the duke bearing a gold cone in honour of the 2012 London Olympics.

ST GEORGE'S GALLER
KELVINSIDE

ST VINCENT PLACE

The city's finest concentration of commercial buildings

Left: This mid-1890s photograph shows St Vincent Place looking towards George Square. The name commemorates Admiral John Jervis's victory in the famous sea battle off Cape St Vincent in 1797. St Vincent Place has the city's finest concentration of commercial buildings, or palazzos as they were called. On the far left is the Italian Renaissance Clydesdale Bank by John Burnet (1874). The intention was to expand the building by adding to the eastern side (to the right in this view), but the *Citizen* newspaper bought the land for its offices and printing works. The red sandstone of T. L. Watson & W. J. Anderson's Citizen Building (1889) was an early example of the Dutch Renaissance style in Glasgow. Further down on the left, at the corner of St Vincent Place and George Square, is the Bank of Scotland by J. T. Rochead (1869). The lamp standard on the right marks the entrance to Glasgow's first fully-equipped gents' underground public lavatory opened in 1892.

Above: While at first glance this view looks much like the previous one, there are changes. On the left, the low building sandwiched between its taller neighbours in the 1890s photo has been replaced with the Anchor Line Building of 1905, an early example of James Miller's penchant for white architecture and his skill in managing to cram seven storeys alongside the neighbouring five. Constructed of white faience carrara (glazed terracotta tiles manufactured by Doulton), the building was unusual for Glasgow. The Anchor Line, founded in 1856 as Handysides and Henderson, was famous for its service between Glasgow and New York and Glasgow and Quebec. Far right are the colossal nine floors of the French inspired former Scottish Provident Building of 1906 designed by J. M. Dick Peddie. The underground toilets are closed, superseded by automated toilet units whose screening came from Glasgow Cross Station when it was demolished.

BUCHANAN STREET

The site of three neighbouring A-listed buildings

Left: On the left of this view of Buchanan Street in the 1950s are three neighbouring A-listed buildings. Far left is the Western Club, established in 1825 when a group of businessmen decided to form a Glasgow club similar to those in London. It moved into the building in 1842, an early example of the Italianate in Glasgow designed by David and James Hamilton in 1839. Alongside is the Gothic Venetian style Stock Exchange founded in 1844. Inspiration for John Burnet Senior's 1875 design is believed to have been that of William Burges's for the London Law Courts. St George's Tron Church, the last of the three A-listed buildings is also the oldest. Designed by William Stark, it opened in 1808 as St George's Parish Church. At that time, the upper section of the street was barely developed and the landmark tower was a significant presence.

Above: While architecturally the three A-listed buildings are unchanged, the usage of two has. In 1965, when the Western Club moved to Royal Exchange Square, its current home, its old building was converted into commercial and retail units. Glasgow Stock Exchange closed in 1973 when it merged with London Stock Exchange and today the building houses commercial, retail and restaurant concerns. The only change for the church is in its name, as in 1940 the Tron St Anne Church united with St George's forming St George's Tron Parish Church. A notable minister was Tom Allan, a key figure in the Scottish evangelical movement in the mid twentieth century. In June 2012 the congregation seceded from the Church of Scotland in censure of the General Assembly's debate on the ordination of openly homosexual ministers.

MUNRO & Co
MAXWELL STREET
HATTERS
Rowan
SCOTSTOUN
632
WEAR
GAELIC
SHOES

ARGYLE STREET

Nowhere in Glasgow was busier than Argyle Street on a Saturday

Left: Argyle Street has always been one of the city's busiest streets and Glaswegians described any place packed to the gunnels as being like Argyle Street on a Saturday. It's had various names – St Enoch's Gait, Dumbarton Road and Westergate. The present one of 1761 honoured Archibald 3rd Duke of Argyll. (Spelling was flexible then.) Pictured here in 1920 is the stretch reaching from Queen Street to the intersection of Jamaica and Union Streets. The building to the right with the arched entry is the Argyll Arcade, Scotland's oldest covered shopping mall (see pages 66–67). The Dutch gabled building right of the tramcar is the Crown Lunch and Tea Rooms, an eighteenth-century building that Kate Cranston had remodelled in 1897 with projecting eaves, gables, and a tower. The basement was turned into a Dutch kitchen with feature fireplace and furnishings designed by Charles Rennie Mackintosh. The domed building belonged to general drapers and warehousemen, Stewart & McDonald Ltd. Ending the vista is the Central Station viaduct.

Above: Projecting on the left is part of the massive St Enoch Centre of 1989. Today, the right-hand side buildings are all freshly painted. There are no sunshades around, but the arcade has a new canopy. Kate Cranston's former tearoom, whose gables and curlicues are seen clearly without a tramcar obstructing them, is now Cranston House. In the 1990s a renovation of the building uncovered the basement fireplace and decorative tiles which were photographed for posterity. At the back of the building in Morrison's Court (1798), entered through an archway within the facade, is the circular spiral staircase tower erected during the 1897 remodelling. Just before the former Stewart & McDonald's is the white Art Deco building of 1938 with zigzags and Egyptian motifs designed for Burton's the Tailors by their architects R. I. Pierce & N. Martin. As before the Central Station viaduct, which by 1997 had been completely refurbished and repainted, closes the vista.

SAINT ENOCH STATION
GLASGOW AND SOUTH WESTERN RAILWAY
GOODS ENTRANCE
WINE MERCHANTS

ST ENOCH STATION AND HOTEL / ST ENOCH CENTRE

The 'most imposing structure in Glasgow' was home to Scotland's largest hotel

Left: St Enoch Station and Hotel is shown here around 1890. The name St Enoch is a corruption of St Thenew – the mother of St Mungo, Glasgow's patron saint. What is now the square was the site of her resting place and a chapel dedicated to her. The first railway bridge across the River Clyde was built in the 1870s and led into St Enoch Station, the terminal of the City of Glasgow Union Railway Co., officially opened in 1876 by the Prince and Princess of Wales (Edward VII and Queen Alexandra). The station shed was the first public area in the city to be regularly lit by electricity. When completed in 1879 the hotel designed by Thomas Wilson was recorded as the 'most imposing structure in Glasgow'. With 200 bedrooms, 20 public rooms and a staff of 80, it was Scotland's largest hotel. In 1883 the hotel and station were acquired by the Glasgow & South Western Railway Co.

Above: St Enoch Station was called 'the happy hunting ground of the golfer' as in addition to courses at Troon, Irvine and Ayr being served by the line, in 1906 the company opened a station and hotel and golf links at Turnberry. By 1910 the station had been out-classed by the Central and following the rationalisation of inter and post-war years, it became increasingly obsolete and in 1966 it closed. Despite the lavishness of the hotel by 1910 the Central Hotel had surpassed it. St Enoch's however, remained a favourite with those who preferred quieter surroundings. During the Second World War it was the headquarters of Naval Intelligence. The hotel stayed open until 1974 when it was closed because of failure to comply with new fire regulations. Despite public outcry and last-ditch attempts to save the building it was demolished in 1977. Here we see what replaced it – the giant glass St Enoch Centre of 1989, nicknamed 'Europe's largest greenhouse'.

St Enoch Square, looking north-west, early 1900s.
St Enoch subway station (1896) is on the extreme left. William and John Costigane's Bonanza Warehouse, an early cut-price store, occupies one of the Square's original eighteenth-century buildings.

ST ENOCH SQUARE

The square's Scotts Renaissance style subway ticket office is now a popular café

Left: This c. 1905 view shows St Enoch Square looking towards Argyle Street. The Bonanza Warehouse was a discount establishment and although patrons were assured of a saving of 25 per cent on all their purchases there was also an assurance that 'good quality is never sacrificed to lowness of price'. At the corner of Argyle Street and Buchanan Street, the towering domed warehouse designed by Horatio Bromhead in 1903 belongs to Stewart & McDonald Ltd. Glaswegians cheekily nicknamed the Atlantes (male figures) supporting the main door 'Stewart and McDonald' after the proprietors. At ground level is H. Samuel's jewellery shop. Just making it into the view on the far left is the enchanting red-sandstone Scots Renaissance style subway ticket office designed by James Miller in 1896, the year the subway opened.

Above: This is a very different perspective of the square than that of the 1900s. A hefty air-monitoring station now sits at the centre of this view. The Bonanza has gone, replaced by what was Arnotts department store, which grew out of a drapery and general warehouse business in Jamaica Street established around 1850 by John Arnott. After amalgamation with the neighbouring store of Robert Simpson the business occupied the entire Jamaica and Argyle Street corner. In 1951 a fire destroyed part of the block and in 1963 rebuilding produced today's building. When Arnotts closed in 1994 the building was split into separate retail units. Stewart & McDonald's huge domed warehouse building is still there but Frasers, a House of Fraser department store, now occupies it. Inset is the former subway ticket office, now occupied by Café Nero.

ARGYLL ARCADE

Scotland's oldest covered shopping centre

Left: The A-listed Argyll Arcade is Scotland's oldest covered shopping centre. It was created by mahogany importer John Reid who commissioned architect John Baird to design a covered walkway lined with shops. Two buildings belonging to the Reid family were to be used as entrances – a tenement in Argyle Street (as it was also sometimes spelt) and one of Buchanan Street's original mansions, photographed here in the 1890s. The arcade's entrance was driven through it. John Baird's use of a hammer-beam roof with iron tie bars was unique among arcades (see inset opposite). When it opened in 1828 it was a highly speculative venture, as at the time Buchanan Street was very much a country road leading to Port Dundas. As it turned out, as well as becoming a centre for quality goods, it helped establish Buchanan Street. On the right is a tea retailing shop opened in 1889 by Stuart Cranston (also spelt Cranstoun), the Glasgow man who invented the tearoom.

Right: In 1894 Stuart Cranston bought the whole arcade and in 1904 replaced the mansion with the French Renaissance style red sandstone Argyll Chambers. One side of the canopy above the entrance spells out the words Argyll Arcade. The other has a coat of arms with the date 1904. The coat of arms belonged to the family of Lord Cranstoun, which had become extinct in 1869. Stuart Cranston had no entitlement to use them. By 1919 money was tight and Cranston was forced to sell parts of the arcade to the tenants. A Committee of Management was appointed and to this day shopkeepers must join it. Any changes in the appearance of the premises must be approved not only by Glasgow's local planning authority, but by the committee. Originally the arcade had a variety of shops, but now, with the exception of two, all are jewellers and the arcade is considered the Hatton Garden of Scotland.

BUCHANAN STREET.

SOUTH END OF BUCHANAN STREET

This once-residential street is now Glasgow's premier shopping thoroughfare

Left: Dated 1901, this image shows Buchanan Street, Glasgow's premier shopping thoroughfare. It was named after tobacco merchant Andrew Buchanan, who in 1766 bought four acres of land reaching from Argyle Street to today's Gordon Street. After building his mansion at what became the south-west corner of Buchanan Street he sold land to form a residential street of mansions. The street changed with the opening of the Argyle Arcade in 1828 (the low building just right of centre). Because the arcade linked Argyle Street with Buchanan Street it encouraged the building of three and four-storey blocks of shops and houses. Left of the arcade is the Prince of Wales Building and Square by John Baird I (1854), a courtyard of business chambers that replaced the street's first house. On the left, a coachman waits outside Wylie & Lochhead's furniture establishment. The covered wagon on the right is parked in front of Wylie Hill's department store.

Above: Today the street looks noticeably the same as it did in 1901, except that it has been pedestrianised and there has been one architectural change. In 1904 the old mansion that fronted the Argyll Arcade was replaced with Argyll Chambers, a red sandstone French Renaissance design block. Next door the Prince of Wales Building is now Princes Square, Britain's leading speciality shopping centre. When it opened in 1987 shoppers were astonished to find that the narrow Buchanan Street entrance opened out to reveal a stunning, four-storey complex. While the walls of the Prince of Wales building formed the sides of the square, a clear glass roof covered the space creating the feeling of a Victorian conservatory. The decoration of the exterior with a sculpture of a giant peacock on the roof is unique to say the least. On the left, Fraser & Sons – now simply Frasers – took over Wylie & Lochhead's establishment.

NESTLE'S
MILK
The Richest in Cream

JAMAICA STREET

Once famous for its collection of iron-framed warehouses

Left: Glasgow's merchants didn't only make fortunes from tobacco, they made them from the lucrative West Indies trade, so when a new thoroughfare was opened at the height of the boom it was aptly named Jamaica Street (1767). This image from the 1880s shows it looking north. It was famous for its collection of early iron-framed warehouses, a form of architecture pioneered in Glasgow. The carriage on the left waits outside the Colosseum Warehouse founded by Walter Wilson in 1869. Born in the Gorbals he started out making ladies' hats and selling them at wholesale prices. He then added more and more departments until he had one of the largest warehouses in the country. Right is R. W. Forsyth Clothier, on the corner of Howard Street, which later moved to the corner of Gordon and Renfield Streets. The horse-drawn trams belong to the Glasgow Tramway and Omnibus Company that entered service in 1872 on track owned by Glasgow Corporation.

Above: All of the buildings from the previous view are gone, leaving no reminder of Glasgow's great engineering past. Only one of the street's cast-iron framed buildings survives. It's not included in the main image but is shown inset. Built in 1856 for cabinet maker and upholsterer A. Gardner & Son, it's the UK's oldest completely cast-iron fronted commercial building. John Baird I designed it with ironwork by R. McConnell, who held the patent for its wrought- and cast-iron beams. The design was the first to apply the principles of Paxton's Crystal Palace – built for the Great Exhibition in London of 1851 – to an everyday building. The business remained in the Gardner family until 1985 when it was acquired by furniture retailer Martin & Frost. With the emergence of companies such as MFI and IKEA it closed and in 2000 the building re-opened as the Crystal Palace bar and restaurant.

PAISLEY'S
STORE
PAISLEY'S

GLASGOW BRIDGE LOOKING NORTH

The view northwards has changed beyond recognition

Left: This colour-tinted photograph shows Glasgow Bridge – also known as Jamaica Bridge – in 1910. It was the third bridge over the crossing. The first was built in 1772, but as it was only 9m (30 ft) wide within the parapets it quickly became incapable of coping with the volume of traffic. Twice it was rebuilt – by Thomas Telford in 1836 with seven arches and in 1891 with four arches. It was later altered to return it to Telford's more elegant seven-arch design. On the far left beside the ship are the piers of the Caledonian Railway Bridge of 1875. Jutting in from the right is the St Enoch Hotel followed by the steeple of St Enoch Church of 1827. The low building left of the steeple is the Custom House designed by John Taylor in 1840. Top left is exclusive outfitters Paisley's Clothiers established in the 1880s.

Above: Today there are no ships moored alongside the bridge. Traffic is one-way southbound and the view northwards has changed beyond recognition. The building on the right-hand corner of the bridge is now a skyscraper that began life as the Royal Stewart Hotel then as Clyde Hall, student accommodation for the university. It's now a Euro Hostel. St Enoch Hotel was demolished in 1977 and replaced with the massive glass covered St Enoch Shopping Centre that opened in 1989. There's no steeple as the St Enoch Church was demolished in 1925. The old Custom House is still there with plans to turn it into a hotel. In the 1980s Hugh Fraser acquired Paisley's renaming it 'Sir Hugh'. The venture failed and the building has been replaced by a red-brick Jurys Inn hotel.

MANUFACTURERS. D.A.GUNN LTD. WAREHOUSEMEN.
BANK OF SCOTLAND
BANK
Golden Shred

GLASGOW BRIDGE LOOKING SOUTH

James Laurie's classical terraces have been restored to their Georgian glory

Left: In 1800 when James Laurie acquired land in the Gorbals he visualised a prestigious suburb with broad classical thoroughfares for the middle and professional classes. He named the district Laurieston after himself and his streets after English nobility. London architect Peter Nicholson designed Carlton Place, which was built between 1802 and 1818. It was named after the Prince Regent's home Carlton House. It consisted of two identical terraces separated by South Portland Street. The western terrace is pictured here in the 1950s when Laurieston and Carlton Place were in decline. Centrepiece in the eastern terrace, the first to be built, was Laurieston House (see top inset), which was actually two houses under one pediment – James living in one, his brother in the other. James's house had the most handsome domestic interior of its date in Glasgow. The internal plasterwork by Francisco Bernasconi who decorated Windsor Castle for George III was sumptuous for the time, as Georgian houses tended to be austere.

Above: When the refurbishment of the terraces began in 1989, it was the biggest single conservation project in Scotland. The exteriors have been restored to their original symmetry and appearance, the roadway has been reinstated with granite setts and pavements have been laid with Caithness stone slabs. On the western terrace, Nos. 71–73 (see bottom inset) were internally remodelled as the Prince and Princess of Wales Hospice, Glasgow's wedding gift to the couple. The hospice relies on the generosity of supporters to raise the £2.8 million required annually to provide free specialist palliative care and support to families throughout a patient's illness. Laurieston House was bought from the council in 1988 by the Strathclyde Preservation Trust who spent £1.6 million on repairs to the foundations and exterior. The trust later sold the house to a private company.

RUBBER
CTURERS.
2

THE 'CA' D'ORO' BUILDING

John Honeyman's Venetian-styled building survived a major fire in 1987

Left: The junction of Union Street and Gordon Street is dominated by the magnificent Venetian-styled, cast-iron palazzo designed by John Honeyman in 1872 as a furniture warehouse. This photograph was taken not long after, probably early in the morning as apart from the shadowy man on the left, a cart, a boy and a man, it's devoid of anything else. Above the giant stone-arched shop fronts, framed by Doric columns, are arched cast-iron windows embellished with decorative mouldings. Behind the iron work the glass seems to form a continuous wall. Circular attic windows are crowned by a concave cornice. The next building along is John Leckie, saddler and portmanteau maker. Next door, in an original mansion, are the offices of the *North British Daily Mail* with beside it Alexander Thomson's four-storey Egyptian Halls of 1871. The tramlines were laid the same year as Honeyman's building was completed.

Above: John Honeyman's building became known as the Ca' d'Oro in 1927 when the City Bakeries opened its magnificent restaurant complex of that name there. Refurbished by J. Gaff Gillespie, one of Glasgow's most avant-garde architects, there was a smoke room and something new – a 'quick service' lunch counter decorated with a view of Venice, a theme continued in the first floor 'Venetian Tea Room'. The Banqueting Hall was on the newly added fifth floor. In its heyday the Ca' d'Oro was a popular venue for weddings until superseded in the 1950s by the Grosvenor in Gordon Street. Although a fire in 1987 destroyed the interior and the concrete mansard of 1927, the cast-iron frame survived. Today's view shows the building reconstructed to its original appearance with the addition of two replica end-bays to Union Street, which replaced the 1920s extension. Thomson's neglected Egyptian Halls are currently shrouded in sheeting printed with an image of the facade.

CENTRAL STATION

The largest public building under glass in the UK

Left: This is a rare photograph of the Central Station in Gordon Street, printed from a 1910 taxiphote, or stereoscopic slide. Prominent is the John Menzies newspaper kiosk and clock. Built for the Caledonian Railway, the station opened in 1879 with eight platforms extended by 1906 to 13. The first Caledonian Railway Bridge (1875) spanning the River Clyde was built just downstream of Glasgow (Jamaica) Bridge. This was replaced in 1905 when the station was enlarged. The piers of the old bridge remain. The glass viaduct crossing Argyle Street is nicknamed the 'Heilanman's Umbrella' by Glaswegians because it was used as a gathering place for visiting Highlanders sheltering from the rain. In 1905 the famous 22m (74ft) long train indicator board appeared. It had a window for each platform, their status being shown by removing a panel from the library of destinations and fixing it to the appropriate window.

Above: A massive refurbishment of the A-listed station began in 1997, the year of its centenary. Work included replacing the magnificent glass roof that stretches from Gordon Street to the River Clyde. The station is the largest public building under glass in the UK. With 50,000 panes of glass and covering six acres, it's three times the size of Hampden Park stadium. The massive timber indicator board has been replaced by a restaurant and shops and now the largest electronic indicator in Europe gives passengers information about departures, arrivals and delays. At the time of its centenary 1,000 trains a day were logged, compared to an average of 600 in 1907. Today, in a year, over 34 million people depart and arrive. Despite changes, like the absence of the landmark John Menzies kiosk and clock, Central Station would still be recognisable to early twentieth-century travellers.

CHRISTIAN INSTITUTE AND YMCA BUILDING

This entire block was demolished in 1980

Left: Photographed in the 1970s, this monumental structure in Bothwell Street was built in three sections over 20 years. The towered first part, built in 1879 as the Christian Institute, arose as a result of the visit to Glasgow in 1874 of evangelists Moody and Sankey. Financed by Rutherglen chemical manufacturer and philanthropist James White, the Institute opened in 1880. Its architect, John McLeod chose German Renaissance as his style, possibly in deference to the Reformation which had its beginnings there. Over the entrance were statues of reformers Knox and Tyndale. In 1895 two massive wings were added, the east containing premises for the Bible Training Institute, the west a restaurant and hostel with 189 beds for the YMCA. Architect R. A. Bryden followed the extravagant style of the first building but with additional towers resulting in an incongruous mixture of styles. The buildings became the headquarters of the city's evangelical movement.

Right: By the time the previous view had been taken, both the Christian Institute and the YMCA had problems with escalating running costs and those of maintaining such a large and complex building. New fire regulations did not help and in 1974 the Glasgow United Evangelistic Association decided to sell the centre and western sections for redevelopment, retaining only the Bible Training Institute to the east. Planning permission was granted on the condition that any new building should match the remaining part. As that was impossible, a decision was made to demolish the whole building that occupied the entire block between West Campbell and Blythswood Streets. This took place in 1980 and the loss to the streetscape was immeasurable. The building that replaced it is more sophisticated than most of the glass-wrapped blocks nearby but it's a poor exchange for the baronial exuberance of the Christian Institute and YMCA building. On the far right, the red sandstone building (built between 1891 and 1901) is the former Central Thread Agency, designed by brothers Hugh and David Barclay for J. & P. Coats.

THEATRE ROYAL

Now home to Scottish Opera and Scottish Ballet

Left: The Theatre Royal in Hope Street, pictured here in the 1920s, is Scotland's longest-running theatre. Originally entered by an arcade in Cowcaddens Street, James Baylis opened it in 1867 as the Royal Colosseum Theatre and Opera House. In 1869 he leased it to William Glover and George Francis who brought the name Theatre Royal with them from their Dunlop Street Theatre Royal, which had been demolished to accommodate St Enoch Railway Station. Following a fire, the auditorium and stage were rebuilt in 1880 to the designs of the renowned theatre architect Charles Phipps. At the same time the entrance was made to face Hope Street. When actor managers Howard & Wyndham took over the running of the theatre in 1888 they announced that in addition to plays, opera and summer shows it would be known principally as a pantomime house. In 1895, when another fire destroyed the auditorium, it was reinstated to Phipps's original design.

Right: On 16 February 1957 the theatre closed with a final performance of *Robinson Crusoe*. Howard & Wyndham Ltd had joined with Roy Thomson of Canada to start commercial television in Scotland with the Royal as the headquarters and studios of Scottish Television. STV was the first sponsor of Scottish Opera – started by Sir Alexander Gibson in 1962 – so when they moved in 1974 to custom-built studios nearby, they offered to sell the theatre to the opera company who bought it with public support. After a lavish refurbishment, Scotland's first national opera house opened in October 1975 with *Die Fledermaus*. Within a few months, the Royal also became the home theatre of Scottish Ballet, which was formed in 1969. Since 1977 the building has been designated A-listed. It's the largest example of Charles Phipps's architecture in Britain. The theatre's domed tower was later replaced by an Italianate centrepiece with a pediment topping.

THEATRE
STAGE DOOR
BUS

C626 CHW

NORTH END OF BUCHANAN STREET

The same view looks unrecognisable today

Left: This photograph shows the north end of Buchanan Street in the mid 1980s. At this time preparations were being made for the construction of a concert hall and shopping centre. The building being demolished is Killermont Street Bus Station. Right of it is ScotRail House built on the site of Buchanan Street Railway Station, which was constructed in 1849 by the Caledonian Railway Company. The station closed in 1966 and the buildings were demolished by 1971. The George Hotel, the shabby building at the end on the left, was built in 1836. It operated as a hotel until the noise from the adjacent building sites made it impossible for residents to get peace. After it closed it had a new purpose – as a film set. With its faded 1950s décor and once-grand fittings, it was in demand with film and television companies. Scenes from *Trainspotting* with Ewan McGregor and *Big Man* with Billy Connolly and Liam Neeson were shot there.

Above: The same view looks unrecognisable today. The only area that helps to orientate the viewer is the left-hand Bath Street corner, which appears behind the pawnbrokers' sign in the 1980s image. Buchanan Street is now closed to the north by the Royal Concert Hall, opened in 1990 as part of Glasgow's tenure as European City of Culture. It was built to replace the St Andrew's Hall at Charing Cross that burned down in 1962. The imposing facade has brought criticism from Glaswegians. Right of the Concert Hall is John Lewis's department store, the company's first in Glasgow. It's the cornerstone of the prestigious Buchanan Galleries shopping centre opened in 1999. Until work started on its construction the site had lain derelict for ten years. Nine escalators and twenty lifts help shoppers negotiate the huge complex. Left is the shopping development that includes the former George Hotel with its facade retained. It is part of the B-listed block that runs from Bath Street round the corner into Sauchiehall Street.

EMPIRE
EMPIRE
SPLENDOUR
GREAT
GLOVE
BARGAINS
WILL HAVE
THE QUICKFIX ELECTRICAL FITTINGS Co 1926
SALE

EMPIRE THEATRE / EMPIRE HOUSE

Lillie Langtry, Laurel and Hardy, Judy Garland and Frank Sinatra all performed here

Left: The legendary Empire Theatre in Sauchiehall Street is shown here in the mid-1930s. Designed by Frank Matcham for Moss Empires, the Glasgow Empire Palace was built on the site of the Gaiety Theatre. When it opened on 5 April 1897, male impersonator Vesta Tilley topped the bill. Quickly establishing itself as Glasgow's leading variety theatre, stars such as Anna Pavlova, Lillie Langtry and Sir Harry Lauder appeared there. On re-opening in 1931, after a refit that made it the second largest variety theatre in Britain, the main attraction was Jack Payne and his BBC Dance Band. When, after the Second World War, top American artistes crossed the Atlantic to perform at the Empire people flocked to see singing and screen idols such as the Andrews Sisters, Ella Fitzgerald, Judy Garland, Johnny Ray, Tony Bennett and Frank Sinatra. On the comedy front were Laurel and Hardy, Dean Martin and Jerry Lewis, Bob Hope and Danny Kaye.

Above: While American performers were ecstatically received, it was when it came to home-grown talent that the Empire earned its reputation as 'the Graveyard of English Comics'. Ken Dodd christened it 'The House of Terror' and disparaged Sigmund Freud's attempts to psychoanalyze humour with the rebuttal, 'He obviously never played second house at the Glasgow Empire after both halves of the Old Firm had just lost.' Glaswegians did not comprehend English humour. Among those who got a hard time were Bob Monkhouse, Tommy Cooper, Mike and Bernie Winters, and Morecambe and Wise. When Des O'Conner's act was jeered it's said he was so overcome by fear that he fainted and had to be carried off. He denied this claiming that the only way to get off the stage in one piece was to pretend to collapse. The farewell show came on 31 March 1963 and the site is now occupied by Empire House, an office development.

ODEON
GEORGE PEPPARD
JAMES MASON
URSULA ANDRESS
THE BLUE MAX
1 20
4 30
7 45
GLOBAL OF LONDON
ODEON

ODEON CINEMA, RENFIELD STREET

Glasgow's Odeon was the most profitable cinema outside of London's West End

Left: This view of the Art Deco Odeon cinema in Renfield Street was taken in 1966. Originally the Paramount, it opened on Hogmanay in 1934 with *She Loves Me Not* starring Bing Crosby and Mary Hopkins. As well as an organ interlude, a stage show was to be included in every Paramount programme, the first featuring Teddy Joyce and his Band. Designed by architects Frank T. Verity and Samuel Beverly for the American Paramount Corporation, it was the only British Paramount cinema north of the border. Occupying half a city block, the facade was white granite with five two-storey finned windows curving around and above the corner entrance. It had a 2m (6ft) high sign and as the whole building had neon 'night architecture' lighting it was a striking landmark. A change of ownership in 1939 brought a name change to the Odeon and during the war it attracted top stars who performed there for war charities.

Above: The Odeon was the best paying cinema outside of London's West End and a popular music venue, which hosted headliners like the Rolling Stones and Bob Dylan. The Beatles were on the same bill as Roy Orbison in June 1963 and in 1965 their only UK tour and the final one as a group, began at the Odeon. By 1970 the cinema had been recreated as the Odeon Film Centre with three screens each showing a different programme. Another three screens were added in 1988 and again in 1999 giving a total of nine. When the Odeon sold the building to property developers in March 2003 Historic Scotland awarded it B-listed status. The end for the Odeon came in 2006 when the sign above the front door said it all: 'Thank you and goodnight ... 31 Dec 34 – 7 Jan 06.' Today the building is in a sorry state and is categorised at 'high risk'.

R·S·McColl
Carswell
NO ENTRY
Sale

CORNER OF RENFIELD AND SAUCHIEHALL STREETS

The Renfield Church of Scotland was one of the few city churches to leave its doors open throughout the week

Left: The corner of Renfield Street and Sauchiehall Street is shown here in the early 1950s. The church is Renfield Street United Presbyterian Church, or the United Presbyterian Cathedral as it was affectionately called. Designed by James Brown and opened in 1848, its style was Perpendicular Gothic with high pinnacles. Despite it setting a new standard for church design in the city, many people thought it too extravagant and it remained without a rival for a number of years. The church became the United Free in 1900 and a Church of Scotland in 1929. R. S. McColl was the most famous name in Glasgow for sweetie shops. The business was begun in 1901 by brothers Robert Smyth McColl and Tom McColl and was named after Robert because he was a football hero, the highlight of his career being a hat-trick in the 4-1 victory over England in 1900.

Above: Renfield Church of Scotland, as it became, was one of the few city churches to keep its doors open during the week for shoppers and passers-by to spend a few quiet minutes in prayer or contemplation. Unfortunately, the cost of maintaining the building became too difficult and in 1964 the church was closed, at which time the congregation united with Milton St Stephen's to form Renfield Parish Church in Bath Street (now known as Renfield Street). Reluctantly, the building was sold for redevelopment and it was demolished in 1965. Today a branch of British Home Stores occupies the whole Renfield/Sauchiehall Street corner site. The McColl brothers sold a controlling interest in their company to the Cadbury Group in 1933 but the name lived on. Today, the shops, now newsagents, are part of the Martin McColl Group, which trades under the R. S. McColl banner in Scotland.

EXHIBITION
QUEENS PARK
942
664

SAUCHIEHALL STREET

Glasgow's most famous thoroughfare

Left: Glasgow's most famous thoroughfare is Sauchiehall Street, whose name derives from it being formed on a 'haugh' or meadow where 'saugh' or willow trees grew. It is therefore a corruption of Sauchiehaugh. This photograph shows the street facing north from the corner of Hope Street and it's easy to date as one of the tramcars is heading for the International Exhibition that was held in Kelvingrove Park in 1901. Electrification of the tramway system had been completed in time for the opening of the exhibition. Right of the tramcars, the imposing red-sandstone building with the arched windows designed by Hugh and David Barclay in 1893 was built for Cumming & Smith, who had built up a successful carpeting and furnishing business in Townhead. The clock tower crowning the tall building on the left belongs to Caledonian House, Copland & Lye's department store designed by James Boucher in 1878.

Above: Today at the left corner of the pedestrianised street is Watt Brothers, Glasgow's last family owned independent department store, which began business there in 1915. While Cumming & Smith's red-sandstone building looks the same, internally it has been greatly changed over the years. The Picture House cinema, opened in December 1910, was created behind the facade. Its luxurious décor incorporated a palm court and two tea lounges, the Wedgewood Room and the Oak Room, making it a highly praised centre of Glasgow social life. The cinema was renamed the Gaumont in 1947 and in January 1954 it introduced Cinemascope to Glasgow when it showed *The Robe*. The Gaumont remained open until 1972, at which time the building was converted into the Savoy Shopping Centre. There's no longer a clock tower on the left. Caledonian House, along with its neighbouring store Pettigrew & Stephens' Manchester House, was demolished in 1973 and replaced with the Sauchiehall Shopping Centre.

GLASGOW SCHOOL OF ART

One of the the world's finest examples of Art Nouveau architecture

Left: This is a seldom-seen view of Glasgow's famous School of Art. Taken around 1900 it shows the building's north facade. Founded in 1845 and based at 116 Ingram Street, the school was known as the Glasgow Government School of Design, until 1853 when it became the Glasgow School of Art. In 1869 it moved to Sauchiehall Street, to a corner of the McLellan Galleries erected in 1855 to accommodate the city's art collection. When Francis Newbery was appointed director in 1885 he oversaw a period of expansion and fast-growing reputation and in 1896 local architects were invited to submit plans for a new building on a site in Renfrew Street. Honeyman & Keppie, where 28-year-old Charles Rennie Mackintosh was a designer, was selected. The building was constructed in two phases. The first, the east end and the main entrance, was built between 1897 and 1899 and the second, the west end, was begun in 1907 and completed in 1909.

Right: Mackintosh's design was eclectic, combining Arts and Crafts and Art Nouveau ethics. As a foil to the rather plain facade there were elaborate iron railings and delicate ironwork at the upper windows. An iron arch spanned the base of the entrance stairs and above the door were stone panels depicting two Art Nouveau female figures above which were two balconies. The west elevation, which ends in steep Scott Street, is said to be the finest piece of architecture for its time anywhere in the world, its oriel windows (shown inset) rising for 20m (65ft). The interior was no less impressive, as Mackintosh was a complete artist – designer, painter, architect and interior designer par excellence. The pièce de résitance was the two-storied library where the use of dark stained timber gave it a Japanese quality. At present, a new campus is being built opposite the Mackintosh Building, which remains as one of the world's finest examples of Art Nouveau architecture.

RENFREW
STREET

THE GRAND HOTEL
CHARING CROSS BRANCH POST OFFICE

CHARING CROSS

Marking the boundary between the city centre and the West End of Glasgow

Left: Situated at the west end of Sauchiehall Street, Charing Cross marks the boundary between the city centre and the West End. It takes its name from London's Charing Cross. On the left in this view of 1897 is the Grand Hotel, Glasgow's most prestigious hotel until the railway companies built luxurious ones next to their stations. Alongside the hotel (far left) is the pink granite and Doulton ware Cameron Memorial Fountain. It was erected in 1896 in recognition of Dublin-born Sir Charles Cameron's services as a Glasgow MP during his first twenty-one years in Parliament. Behind the hotel is the magnificent French Renaissance style Charing Cross Mansions of 1889-91 designed by J. J. Burnet with a tall galleried cupola and a clock surrounded by carved figures. It was the first time in the city that red sandstone was used for a building of this scale.

Above: The Grand Hotel was a popular venue for wedding receptions and dances and as it was convenient for the west-end theatres it was in demand for those frequenting them. During the Second World War, the American Red Cross took over the hotel as a club for US Forces on leave in Scotland. After the war it became run-down and despite opposition, it was demolished in 1969 to make way for the M8 motorway that devastated the area around Charing Cross. As this image shows, the loss of the Grand left the view to the east open to the landmark Charing Cross Mansions that curve from Sauchiehall Street into Renfrew Street. Prominent is the colourful Cameron Fountain, often referred to as Glasgow's equivalent to the Leaning Tower of Pisa due to subsidence caused by traffic over the decades.

CHURCH TOWERS FROM LYNDOCH PLACE

One of the most exhilarating skylines in Glasgow

Left: Lyndoch Place offers one of Glasgow's most exhilarating skylines: the towers of Park Parish Church, Free Church College and the twin towers of the College Church. While all four towers are in this view from the early 1960s, dominant is that of Park Church, designed by J. T. Rochead in 1857. The interior was a departure for a Church of Scotland building as it had a chancel, communion table, stained glass and no galleries. The tower was an adaptation of West of England Perpendicular architecture. Right of the church is the galleried campanile of the Free Church College of 1857 designed by Charles Wilson. Left are the Romanesque twin towers of the adjoining College Church. Following the union of the Free Church and the United Presbyterian Church in 1900, College Church became the Glasgow College of the United Free Church of Scotland. When fire destroyed the church in 1903 it was rebuilt and incorporated into the college as its library.

Above: Following the union of the United Free Church and the Church of Scotland in 1929, the college was renamed Trinity College, which merged with the Faculty of Divinity at the University of Glasgow in 1935. Classes were divided between the university and the college, a practice which continued – apart from during the Second World War when the building was occupied by the Royal Pay Corps – until 1973 when all classes were transferred to the university. The former college building has since been converted into flats. The major change here is that while the Park Church tower remains, the church itself has gone. Before its demolition in 1969 the outcry was great and there was heated debate between the Church of Scotland and preservationists. The church won and as a compromise the tower was retained. The modern building that replaced it is a blot on the Park District, one of the finest examples of Victorian planning in Britain.

ST VINCENT STREET CHURCH

Alexander 'Greek' Thomson's masterpiece

Left: This 1870s photograph shows St Vincent Street Church, Alexander Thomson's masterpiece of 1857–59 designed for the United Presbyterian Church. Rejecting the Gothic Revival style of the time, he gained his inspiration from the classical architecture of Ancient Greece. Built on a steep slope, the structure is placed on a massive podium containing the lower part of the church and the basement. The upper part is in the form of a large Greek temple with six fluted columns supporting a portico. The powerful tower encompasses elements from a number of countries including Egypt, India and Assyria. Internally, the church was sumptuous and well lit with bright red, blues and greens on columns, capitals and friezes, surprisingly flamboyant for a Presbyterian place of worship. In 1900 it became a United Free Church of Scotland and in 1929 a Church of Scotland. In the 1960s the building was purchased by Glasgow Corporation.

Right: In 1886 the congregation of the Free Church purchased Ewing Place Congregational Church at the corner of Waterloo Street and West Campbell Street. They worshipped there until 1957 when a fire destroyed it. From then the congregation had no permanent home, until 1971 when it leased the St Vincent Street Church from the Corporation. In 1994 when the Milton Free Church amalgamated with the St Vincent Street Church the congregation became known as St Vincent Street-Milton Free Church of Scotland. In 2009, to reflect more accurately its vision and mission in the twenty-first century, the name was changed to Glasgow City Free Church. When it was listed in the 1998 World Monuments Watch by the World Monuments Fund and again in 2004 and 2006, the fund helped restore the tower. The building is the only complete church by Alexander Thomson to survive and despite being surrounded by high-rise office blocks it still dominates the area.

KELVINGROVE ART GALLERY AND MUSEUM

Scotland's busiest tourist attraction served as the Palace of Fine Arts for the Glasgow International Exhibition of 1901

Left: Dated 1901, this photograph shows the Kelvingrove Art Gallery and Museum. With its exotic towers and vivid colouring, it is many Glaswegians' favourite building. Planning began in 1886 when the city decided to build a combined art gallery and museum to house all its collections under one roof. Construction was financed by the proceeds of the 1888 International Exhibition in Kelvingrove Park. The style chosen by English architects J. W. Simpson and E. J. Milner Allen was Spanish Baroque. That the building was erected back to front and that one of the architects committed suicide by jumping from one of the towers when he realised his mistake is a myth. It was designed to face into Kelvingrove Park. For further funding, another International Exhibition was planned and when it opened in May 1901 the magnificent new building served as the Palace of Fine Arts where its brilliant red sandstone facade provided a dramatic contrast to James Miller's white and gold main exhibition hall.

Above: After the exhibition, it took time to return the loan collections exhibited and it was not until 25 October 1902 that the Kelvingrove Art Gallery and Museum formally opened. While collections mainly came from the McLellan Galleries and the old Kelvingrove House Museum, over the decades wealthy Glaswegians bequeathed treasures such as an armoury collection, one of the best in the world. In 1952 the museum purchased Salvador Dali's *Christ of St John of the Cross* for £8,200. Now worth around £70 million, out of all the impressive art works exhibited, including a Rembrandt and a Van Gogh, it's the picture every visitor wants to see. After a three-year closure for a major renovation, Kelvingrove reopened on 11 July 2006 and in 2011 it was voted the UK's best Scottish Museum, knocking Edinburgh Castle off the top spot as Scotland's busiest tourist attraction.

STEWART MEMORIAL FOUNTAIN

Commemorating Robert Stewart who brought fresh water to Glasgow

Left: The Stewart Memorial Fountain, pictured here around 1885, was erected in Kelvingrove Park in 1872. James Sellars was the architect and John Mossman the sculptor. It commemorates Provost Robert Stewart who was instrumental in 1859 with the delivery of Glasgow's water supply from Loch Katrine. This provided clean and fresh drinking water for the citizens, eradicating the threat of cholera and typhus. Built of granite, sandstone, marble and bronze, the prominent feature was a crown topped by a tall, gilded bronze statue of The Lady of the Lake, the subject of a poem by Sir Walter Scott. Below the statue were lions and unicorns holding shields. Other decorations included signs of the zodiac and features relating to the natural history of the Trossachs, the location of Loch Katrine. Decorating the base were plaques containing a bust of Stewart, Glasgow's coat of arms and the arms of Scotland. Left is the university with its unfinished tower that was completed in1891.

Above: Over the decades the fountain had effectively become a climbing frame used by vandals. Many of the grotesques, birds and nearly all of the fountain nozzles had been removed, damaging the stonework. In 2005 Land and Environmental Services Parks and Scottish Water agreed to fund its restoration. On 14 October 2009 – the 150th anniversary of the day fresh water flowed into Glasgow for the first time – a restored Stewart Memorial Fountain was unveiled by Lord Provost Winter. There's no doubt that the bringing of clean water was primarily responsible for ridding the city of cholera and typhus epidemics. In the British epidemic of 1866 only 55 lives were lost in Glasgow, as compared to 4,000 in the 1832 epidemic. In its original state, the fountain only operated at prescribed times, as to run it continuously was unsustainable. The new re-circulation system has enabled it to operate sustainably and continuously for the first time in its history.

UNIVERSITY OF GLASGOW

Gilmorehill was the university's third location

Left: This photograph of Glasgow University on Gilmorehill was taken from Kelvin Way in 1889. It is easy to date as on the left are remnants of the 1888 International Exhibition held in Kelvingrove Park. The castle-like building far left was a representation of the former Bishops' Palace in Castle Street. When the university was established in 1451 classes were held in Glasgow Cathedral's Lower Church. In the seventeenth century it moved into what was known as the 'Old College' in High Street. When this became unsuitable it moved to Gilmorehill in 1870. The Gothic-style main structure by Sir George Gilbert Scott consisted of buildings arranged around two quadrangles separated by the Bute and Randolph Halls. The vaulted cloisters beneath the halls and the landmark Flemish-style central tower were completed by J. Oldrid Scott, as his father had died in 1878. Pearce Lodge of 1888 (see inset above) incorporates salvaged features of the Old College Gateway.

Above: The university's main south staircase led to Scotland's oldest museum, the Hunterian, which contained the bequeathed collections of anatomist and physician William Hunter (1718–83). When changes in teaching methods and the introduction of new subjects strained accommodation, new buildings were required and the first extension beyond the main building was the Botanical Building of 1901. With a need for further accommodation, in 1909 it was decided to complete the West Quadrangle and to include a university chapel. However, it was not until 1929 that Sir John Burnet's War Memorial Chapel was dedicated to the 733 members of the university who died in the First World War. Obscured by trees, to the right is the university's circular reading room of 1939 that replaced Hillhead House. Alongside is the 12-storey library, begun in 1968 and extended in the 1980s and 1990s. It formed the centrepiece of the new campus buildings built across Hillhead during the 1960s.

KELVIN BRIDGE (GREAT WESTERN ROAD BRIDGE)

Three bridges have crossed the River Kelvin here

Left: This late 1860s image shows the first and second Kelvin bridges. Previously at this point the river was crossed by Hillhead Ford. Approached over poor roads, the lower zig-zag bridge was built in 1825. It was a low-level, roughly built, four-arched masonry structure only 4.2m (14ft) above the river bed and only 5m (16ft) wide. Surmounting it is the high-level, four-arch toll bridge of 1840 that carried Great Western Road across the river. The road had been formed by an Act of Parliament in 1836 that authorised the construction of the Great Western Turnpike from St George's Cross to Anniesland Toll. To the left of the bridge is the cast-iron parapet of the extension built to carry the Loch Katrine water pipes. Alongside the bridge is Lansdowne Church designed by John Honeyman in 1862 and which has the most slender church spire in Glasgow. The white cottage on the right belonged to the South Woodside mills.

Right: The two previous bridges remained open until a third bridge, today's, was fully completed. Opened in 1891, the present Kelvin Bridge can be crossed almost unnoticed because its road is level with the streets at both ends. For a time after its opening it was jokingly known as the 'tombstone bridge' because of the four panels on each side bearing the names of the councillors forming the committee concerned with its construction. The names were later removed. Decorating the inside parapets are three badges bearing the arms of Glasgow, Lanarkshire and Hillhead. Hidden below the bridge's deck are the huge pipes which bring water from Loch Katrine. There are major changes between this view and that of the 1860s. The old bridges and cottages have gone and beyond Lansdowne Church is the spire of St Mary's Episcopal Cathedral, designed as a parish church by Sir George Gilbert Scott in 1871.

BOTANIC GARDENS

Including the magnificent A-listed Kibble Palace conservatory

Left: This early 1890s view shows the Botanic Gardens in Great Western Road. They evolved from the Physic Garden in the Old College in High Street, which the Royal Botanical Institution of Glasgow relocated west to Fitzroy Place in 1815. Looking for purer air, the gardens were moved to today's site in 1842. Initially they were private and exclusive, but later the public was admitted on selected days on payment of one old penny. On the right is the Kibble Palace, named after John Kibble who had the magnificent conservatory built at his home in Coulport, Loch Long in 1865. He moved it to the Botanic Gardens in 1873 where he used it as a concert hall. Important meetings were also held there, including the rectorial addresses delivered to Glasgow University students by Gladstone and Disraeli. In 1891 the gardens and the Kibble Palace became the property of the Corporation. On the left is one the Main Range glasshouses of 1888.

Above: Nestling among the planting are marble statues that were moved to the Kibble Palace from Kelvingrove Museum in the late 1930s. The centrepiece is *Eve* sculpted in 1880 by Scipione Tadolini. Between 1988 and 2004 a phased restoration of the B-listed Main Range glasshouses took place beginning with the Palm House. On 29 September 2003 the Kibble Palace closed for a £7 million major restoration that involved the complete dismantling of the building. Over the winter of 2003–04 all the plants were removed with many being stored off site for the duration of the restoration. The A-listed Kibble Palace, one of the most prestigious iron and glass structures remaining from Victorian times, re-opened on St Andrew's Day 2006. Among the plants returned were the Australasian tree ferns that had been growing there for 120 years and were of international importance. Today, the beautifully restored building attracts thousands of visitors.

WHOLESALE
LEATHER WAREHOUSE
236
CHAMOIS SPONGES
BELTS & RAZOR STROPS
WHOLESALE & RETAIL
LEATHER MERCHANT
ASTRY BAKER

CALTON ENTRY

Houses were demolished in the 1930s to make way for the Barrowland Ballroom

Left: These old houses were situated at what was called the Calton Entry in the Gallowgate, one of Glasgow's eight original streets. The name Calton comes from a 'hazel grove' in old Scots and Gallowgate was the way to the gallows. In 1730 merchant John Orr bought the estate and five years later King George II made it a Barony with a right to make laws and punish those who broke them, irrespective of any control from the neighbouring city. The houses shown in this 1903 view were probably built around 1750, a prosperous time for building plots to be taken up. In common with city architecture at the time, one of the houses had a Dutch-style chimney gable. Calton is ever identified with weaving and the history of its weavers was turbulent, the strike against wage cuts in 1787 being the most notable when it culminated with three weavers being killed by soldiers.

Above: The old houses remained until the early 1930s when they were demolished to make way for the famous Barrowland Ballroom. The weekend market or 'Barras' as it is popularly known, began in the early 1920s when Maggie and James McIver began renting out barrows to hawkers around Gallowgate. When several tenements were demolished in the area, the McIvers bought the ground to use as a permanent market site. After the marketplace was covered over in 1926 and completely enclosed by 1931, Maggie decided to build a function suite for the traders to use. On Christmas Eve 1934, Barrowland Ballroom opened. After a fire in 1958, a new building was erected and officially re-opened on Christmas Eve 1960. The tenement on the right, lowered into a single storey, houses Baird's Bar. Two of Gallowgate's nearby crow-stepped tenements built in 1771 have been renovated, No. 394 and No. 379, housing the Heilan Jessie pub.

RMARY

DAVID DALE HOUSE

Dale's Robert Adam mansion has been replaced by a Le Corbusier style complex

Left: In 1779 David Dale and Archibald Paterson laid out Charlotte Street, which ran north and south between Glasgow Green and the Gallowgate, intersected by London Road. While the north part of the street was to consist of tenements for artisans the south end was to contain elegant mansions each with a coach house and garden. Dale secured a prime site at the south-west corner in 1780 where he built the largest house in the street, shown here around 1890. Designed by Robert Adam in Palladian style, it cost more than £6,000, which he could well afford as his business interests included linen yarn importing, dye works and coal mining. He was an agent for the Royal Bank, a founder member of the Glasgow Chamber of Commerce and in 1786, along with Richard Arkwright, he founded the large cotton spinning mill and progressive weaving community at New Lanark. Dale left Charlotte Street in 1800 to live in Rosebank in Cambuslang.

Above: Dale's family sold the house in 1827 and in the 1850s it housed the Glasgow Eye Infirmary, where Dr William McKenzie carried out eye operations in Dale's octagonal library with its fine domed roof. The infirmary relocated to the West End in 1874 and subsequently the building became a Salvation Army Men's Home. Amid much controversy, Dale's house was demolished in 1954 to make way for an extension to Our Lady and St Francis School, which dated from 1847 when the first Franciscan Sisters to come to Glasgow settled in Charlotte Street and opened a girls' school attached to their convent. The extension shown here was designed by Gillespie, Kidd & Coia in 1964. Inspired by Le Corbusier, this A-listed building is now the headquarters of The Wise Group, a social enterprise that makes an impact on people, communities and society. Of the original mansions, the only one that remains (see inset) was converted into flats by the National Trust for Scotland.

DOULTON FOUNTAIN

The world's largest three-storey terracotta fountain

Left: Designed by Arthur Edward Pearce, the A-listed Doulton Fountain is the world's largest three-storey terracotta fountain. It was the principal exhibit at the Glasgow International Exhibition of 1888 in Kelvingrove Park and was a personal gift to the city by Sir Henry Doulton. It was relocated to Glasgow Green and its inauguration on 27 August 1890 was designated as a special 'fountain day'. This photograph looking west shows it in 1891. A figure of Queen Victoria as Empress of India bearing orb and sceptre surmounted the structure. Water pouring from the urns of four kneeling maiden figures passed four others representing the Black Watch, the Royal Navy, the Royal Irish Fusiliers and the Grenadier Guards. It then fell into a large cantilevered basin from where it exited through the mouths of 12 lion masks, bypassing colonial figures representing India, Canada, South Africa and Australia to land in the outer basin.

Above: In 1894 the figure of Queen Victoria was destroyed by lightning. Rather than let the city replace it with a cheaper urn, Doulton paid for a second figure himself. It had to be craftsman-made when it was discovered that the original moulds had been broken-up. Given the fountain's fragile composition it had always been vulnerable to damage and in the 1970s, when it was showing signs of deterioration due to weathering and vandalism, it was fenced off, the lower basin supported by scaffolding and much of the statuary removed for safe-keeping. In the mid-1990s, as part of a regeneration scheme for Glasgow Green, attention was turned to it and on 9 May 2005, following a £3.75 million refurbishment and relocation in front of the People's Palace Museum and Winter Gardens (1898), a gloriously restored Doulton Fountain was ceremoniously switched on by the Lord Provost.

TEMPLETON'S FACTORY

This iconic Glasgow building was based on the Doge's Palace in Venice

Left: This photograph of 1900 shows Templeton's carpet factory completed in 1892. Architect William Leiper modelled the spectacular Venetian Gothic facade on the Doge's Palace in Venice. Facing Glasgow Green, the main elevation was a riot of terracotta inlaid with red, deep blue, green and white enamel mosaic topped with a golden carpet-like frieze. The colours were chosen to mimic the brilliance of the carpets woven by Templeton. Glasgow builder James Goldie was responsible for the exquisite brickwork and for years bricklayers' apprentices were brought to study his techniques. Tragedy struck during construction. On 1 November 1889 at 5.15 p.m., a severe gust of wind caught an unsecured wall that collapsed on top of the weaving sheds connected to the old mill. There were 140 people working in the sheds and although it was feared that 50 weavers had lost their lives the final death toll was 29, mostly young girls.

Above: As Templeton became the largest manufacturer of quality carpets in the British Empire, the factory was expanded in the 1920s and 30s by George Boswell. In homage to William Leiper, Boswell used coloured brickwork and tiles but in an Art Deco style. In the 1920s Charles Rennie Mackintosh and his wife Margaret MacDonald collaborated with the company on innovative and original textile designs, known internationally as 'The Glasgow Style'. Templeton provided the carpeting for the coronations in 1911, 1937 and 1953. On merging with Stoddard Carpets in 1980 the factory closed and in 1984 it became the Templeton Business Centre. Erected in 2005, Templeton Gate, just out of view on the left, commemorates the girls who died at the factory. The story is carved in the light section of stone across the base of the gate. The A-listed building is so iconic that it featured on a stamp in 1990 when Glasgow was the European City of Culture.

AND
CARRIAGE

BRIDGETON CROSS

This A-listed Victorian shelter is one of the best preserved of its kind

Left: In the East End of the city, the junction at Bridgeton Cross is the meeting point of London Road, Dalmarnock Road, Main Street, James Street, Olympia Street and Orr Street. In 1875 a shelter was built at the cross for homeless people. Affectionately known as the Umbrella, the open-sided octagonal cast-iron shelter, manufactured by George Smith & Co at their Port Dundas Sun Foundry, had a bright red shingle roof topped with a square clock and fancy weathervane. Behind it the Caledonian Railway Company's Bridgeton Cross Station that opened in 1872. Also provided by the foundry was the cherub-topped drinking fountain left of the cab. This 1894 photograph shows that the shelter was popular, not only for the disadvantaged, but as a general congregating spot.

Above: The shelter eventually became a haunt for drunks and other addicts and in 1995 the seats were removed in an attempt to stop people loitering there. As this view shows, apart from the shelter all the buildings in the 1894 shot have vanished. Instead of the Caledonian Railway Company's station there's the former Olympia Theatre of Varieties, opened in 1911 in the impressive red sandstone building designed by John Arthur with an auditorium by Frank Matcham. (Inset is a poster of 1912.) After the First World War the theatre changed to cine-variety and in 1924 to a full-time cinema. In latter years it became a bingo hall and then a furniture shop, until 1993 when it was abandoned. In 2011 a major restructuring of the Olympia as a community facility was begun and this photograph shows it almost completed. The Umbrella was restored to its previous grandeur in 2010. It's one of the rarest and best quality examples of its kind anywhere in the UK and for that reason is A-listed.

TOLLCROSS HOUSE

This baronial mansion was built for landowner and industrialist James Dunlop

Left: This photograph of 1910 shows Tollcross House situated in Tollcross Park in the East End of Glasgow. David Bryce designed the Scots baronial mansion built in 1848 for James Dunlop, the owner of Tollcross Estate and proprietor of the Clyde Ironworks. Among the accommodation was a drawing room, a dining room, a library and 23 bedrooms. James Dunlop went bankrupt in 1889 and after his death in 1893 it was suggested that the house and estate would be useful as a public park. Glasgow Corporation acquired 83.5 acres of land, including the house for £29,000 and in June 1897 the Lord Provost performed the opening ceremony of Tollcross Park. In 1905, a Children's Museum was opened in the house, the most popular exhibit being the Cock Robin display, containing a selection of preserved birds arranged in a glass case depicting the nursery rhyme *Who Killed Cock Robin?*

Above: Due to financial strictures, the Children's Museum closed at the beginning of the 1970s. The building was in an advanced state of disrepair and was closed entirely in 1973. In 1992 the National Trust for Scotland undertook its renovation, restoring it back to its original grandeur at a cost of around £2 million with assistance from the local authority and other funding sources. In the same year the building was acquired by Shettleston Housing Association which contracted with the Church of Scotland Board of Responsibility to provide a registered sheltered housing complex for older people. Today the A-listed house, consisting of seven shared and four single occupancy flats provides 24-hour supported living to people aged 65 and over. The main image does not show the house from the same viewpoint as the 1910 photo, as it is now obscured by trees (see inset).

NO BILLS
WINE, SPIRIT
VAULTS.

GORBALS

Main Street (now Gorbals Street) has been redeveloped beyond recognition

Left: At first Gorbals, or Bridgend as it was commonly known, was a single street village that expanded after completion of a bridge over the River Clyde in 1345. The Church controlled the lands and after the Reformation Archbishop Boyd feued the village to George Elphinstone, who built a baronial mansion and tower adjoining St Ninian's Chapel in Main Street. By the end of the eighteenth century street plans were calling the village 'Gorbells' instead of Bridgend. Weaving was its main industry and there were at least 60 public houses that, according to the minister, 'hurt the morals of the people not a little'. By the second half of the nineteenth century the village was a crowded, crumbling slum and along with similar areas the City Improvement Trust demolished it. This view of Main Street in 1868 looking north was taken when St Ninian's Chapel (far right) was a pub and Elphinstone Tower (next door) had been divided into flats.

Above: The redeveloped area remained the heart of Gorbals. Main Street, leading to Victoria Bridge was realigned and straightened and Gorbals Cross, begun in 1872, was the focal point with the corners angled to create a diamond shape. Alexander Thomson designed the building that formed the north-west corner. In 1878 an ornate cast-iron clock, public drinking fountain and underground public conveniences were erected at the centre of the cross (shown inset in the 1920s). While Gorbals thrived as a community of various immigrant groups, through time there were problems of building decay, overcrowding and poor sanitation and in the 1950s work began on regeneration, mainly by building high-rise flats. This was unsuccessful and they were demolished and replaced with low-level housing. Main Street (now Gorbals Street) was completely rebuilt and the area shown in the previous view now houses the Glasgow and Strathkelvin Sheriff Court and the Glasgow Central Mosque and Islamic Centre.

GORBALS

Almost every architectural reference point south of the river has disappeared since the 1960s view

Left: This aerial view shows the Victorian Gorbals Cross, with corners angled to create a diamond shape – visible just left of centre in the foreground. At the time of this 1966 photo the area was about to undergo massive regeneration. Gorbals Street (old Main Street) leads north to the Victoria Bridge of 1851, the city's oldest bridge. To the right is the City Union Railway Bridge of 1897 leading to St Enoch Station. On the left of Victoria Bridge is the 1864 clipper HMS *Carrick*, originally the *City of Adelaide*, which conveyed countless emigrants to Australia. The spire far left on the south of the river belongs to Gorbals Parish Church. Designed by David Hamilton in 1806, the top of the spire was removed after it was struck by lightning in 1930. Right of the church is Buchan Street School dating from the 1870s. The chimney on the right-hand side of Gorbals Street belongs to the Adelphi Distillery.

Above: This modern view bears very little relation to the previous one. Apart from a couple of buildings everything south of the river has been demolished. Where Gorbals Cross was is now the intersection of Gorbals, Ballater and Norfolk Streets. To the left in the foreground, high-rise housing replaces the tenements. To the right is the low-rise housing erected when the area was regenerated for the third time. The Adelphi Distillery has been replaced with the Glasgow Central Mosque and Islamic Centre, with its 5m (16ft) tall minaret, completed in 1986. It replaced a temporary building in the Gorbals that had been established in the 1940s. David Hamilton's church and Buchan Street School have been replaced by Glasgow and Strathkelvin Court, dating from 1980–86. Containing 21 courtrooms, it's said to be the second largest court in Europe. The *Carrick* now lies rotting next to the Scottish Maritime Museum in Irvine.

CALEDONIA ROAD CHURCH

Alexander Thomson's Greek Revival edifice still marks the corner of Cathcart Road and Gorbals Street

Left: Caledonia Road Church in the Gorbals is shown here on its gushet, or wedged, site in c. 1860. It was designed in 1856 by Alexander Thomson for the United Presbyterian congregation. He was an elder of the church, had a family pew there and it was where he worshipped until his death in 1875. He's buried in the Southern Necropolis near the church. Thomson's design for the building was Greek Revival. Its Ionic pillared portico was raised 7m (23ft) onto an artificial acropolis, which at the same time formed the vestibule. His inspiration for the tower came from Renaissance churches in Italy's Lombardy region. The interior woodwork and plastered walls were covered with stencilled patterns in red, green and gold. As a whole, the building was an unusual design for a Free Church, normally noted for the austere simplicity of its buildings. In 1857 Thomson designed the adjoining blocks of tenements which completed the triangular site.

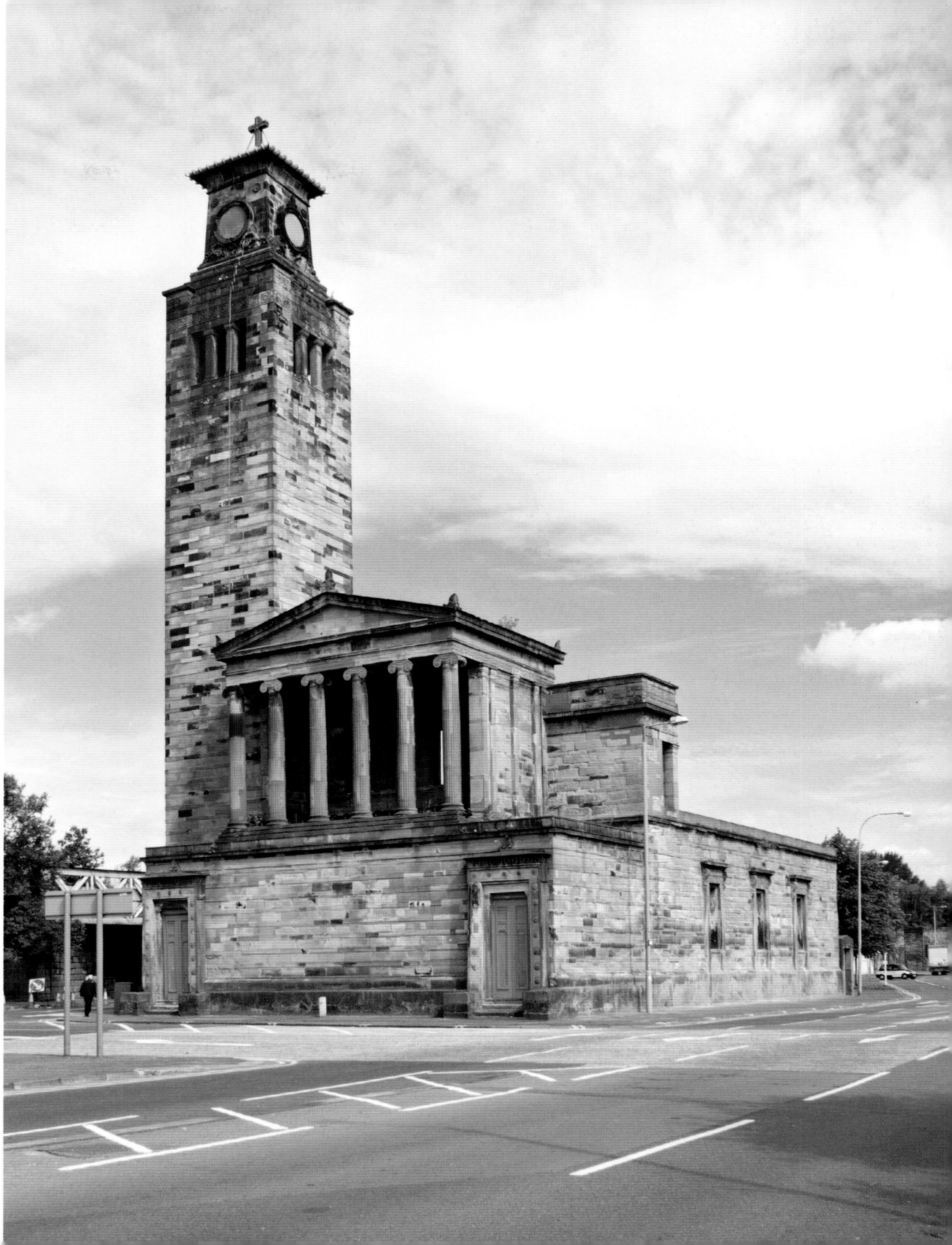

Right: Subsequently the church became Caledonia Road United Free and in 1924 the congregation united with Hutchesontown United Free as Hutchesontown and Caledonia Road UF. Declining membership and population in the area resulted in the church closing in 1962. A year later the Church of Scotland sold it to Glasgow Corporation who carried out remedial repairs. In 1964 when a survey revealed that full restoration would cost around £90,000, an option considered was to dismantle the structure and rebuild it elsewhere. Both the Church and the Corporation were willing to contribute to the estimated cost of £150,000 but the plan was thwarted when the Historic Buildings Council refused to help. When vandals set fire to the church in 1965 only the burned out shell remained. Stabilisation of the A-listed structure was completed in 1969 and today, marooned by traffic, it stands like a sentinel at the junction of Cathcart Road and Gorbals Street. Thomson's tenements were demolished in the 1970s.

CITIZENS' THEATRE

The classical facade has gone but the theatre remains

Left: Main Street Gorbals had two theatres in adjoining buildings and they are both pictured in this 1960s image. The oldest one opened in 1878 as Her Majesty's Theatre, with a classical facade that had been the portico of the old Union Bank in Ingram Street. Architect James Sellars modified it to fit its new setting and added six statues to the parapet – four muses, flanked by Shakespeare and Burns. Within six months the theatre had closed and in 1879 it re-opened as the Royal Princess's, presenting melodrama, variety and pantomime. The pantomimes were distinguished by always having 13 letters in their title, such as *Tammie Toddles*. In September 1945 the Royal Princess's became the Citizens' Theatre. Sharing the Royal Princess's columned facade was the Palace Theatre that opened in 1904. By 1914, however, it was offering a mixture of films and variety acts that continued until 1930 when films took over entirely. The Palace cinema closed in 1962 and became a bingo hall.

Right: Led by playwright James Bridie, the Citizens' Theatre Company was formed in 1943 to provide a medium for Scottish plays using Scottish actors. It had taken a ten-year lease on the Royal Princess's Theatre. On its expiry in 1955 Glasgow Corporation purchased the theatre and leased it back to the company. In 1977 the Palace bingo hall was subject to a demolition order and before action could be taken it was bulldozed along with the shared facade. Fortunately, the statues and some original features were saved. The Citizens got the yellow brick facade shown here in 1989. Behind is the Royal Princess's B-listed Victorian interior. Today, the theatre consists of three theatrical spaces: the Main Theatre seating 459, the Circle Studio which seats 90 and the Stalls Studio which seats 45. The statues of the four muses, Shakespeare and Burns are in the foyer.

CITIZENS
EATRE CITIZENS THEATRE CITIZENS THEATRE CITIZEN
ARE YOU SITTING COMFORTABLY?
THE MONSTER
THE HALL
TWO SMASH HIT PLAYS
citz.co.uk
AUTUMN 2012
COMING SOON TO THE CITIZENS THEATRE
ON SALE NOW!
YELLOW MOON & THE MONSTER IN THE HALL
GLASGOW GIRLS THE MUSICAL
TAM O'SHANTER
SLEEPING BEAUTY
MEDEA
TAKIN' OVER THE ASYLUM

BATTLEFIELD MONUMENT

Alexander Skirving's column marks the site of the Battle of Langside

Left: Battlefield Monument in Battle Place, Langside, is shown here c. 1890. It commemorates the Battle of Langside fought on 13 May 1568 between the forces of Mary Queen of Scots and those of Regent Moray. Moray's troops were positioned on Langside Hill while Mary's were on the lesser Clincart Hill (now the site of Langside College). Mary's forces approached Lang Loan (now Battlefield Road) and the two armies clashed roughly where the monument stands. Mary watched from Cathcart Hill (now known as Court Knowe). In only 45 minutes her troops were defeated with over 300 killed. Mary fled to England, to imprisonment and eventual execution in 1587. The B-listed monument, designed by Alexander Skirving with sculptures by James Young, was erected in 1887. The lion at the top rests his paw on a cannonball and faces Clincart Hill. Spiralling up the column is a design of thistles, roses and fleur-de-lis reflecting Mary's coat of arms.

Above: The monument now stands on an island at a busy road junction. When it was stone-cleaned and restored in 1987, a plaque was put up explaining that the Battle of Langside was fought there. Behind the monument is the A-listed former Langside Free Church. Designed by Alexander Skirving in 1894, it was the last classical church to be built in Glasgow. The Earl of Moray, whose ancestors had fought Queen Mary at the battle, laid the foundation stone on 21 September 1895. The style of the church, described as a free adaptation of Greco-Roman and imposingly placed on a large plinth and fronted by a pedimented portico supported by Ionic columns, was obviously influenced by Alexander Thomson, as Skirving was his chief draughtsman. The church closed in 1979 and after years of neglect it opened as a pub and restaurant in 1990.

HAMPDEN PARK

The world's first international football stadium

Left: Hampden Park in Mount Florida is shown here in the 1950s. It was the world's first international football stadium and surprisingly was built for an amateur team, Queen's Park. There have been three Hampden Parks, this one being the third. The first situated alongside Prospecthill Road was opened in 1873. Ironically, it was called Hampden after the terrace opposite named after John Hampden, a seventeenth-century English Parliamentarian. When the Cathcart railway line was planned to cut through its ground the club relocated to Cathcart Road to the second Hampden. When this became too small, ground was bought in Somerville Drive on which the third Hampden Park, the world's biggest and most technically advanced stadium, was built. The opening game was on 31 October 1903 when Queen's Park beat Celtic 1–0. The first international attended by 102,741 people was on 7 April 1906 when Scotland beat England 2–1. This match established Hampden as the primary home of the Scotland team.

Above: Over the years attendances increased and when Queen's Park purchased more land in 1923, 25,000 more places were added to the terraces with rigid crush barriers being installed in 1927. The Scotland v England match in 1937 set a European all-time international record. The official attendance was 149,415 but at least 20,000 more people entered the ground without tickets. Still remembered as the greatest game ever was the European Cup final between Real Madrid and Eintracht Frankfurt in 1960, when Real defeated Eintracht 7–3 to be crowned Europe's greatest side for the fifth consecutive season. By the late 1970s Hampden was crumbling and in the 1980s the government went back on a promise to help refurbish it. In 1993, however, redevelopment began and in 1999 a new state-of-the-art stadium was unveiled. It houses the world's first football museum and offices for the Scottish Football Association, the Scottish Premier League and Scottish Football League.

POLLOK HOUSE

The Pollok estate was owned by the Maxwell family for seven centuries

Above: Pollok House is set within Pollok Country Park, three miles south of the city centre. The Pollok estate came into the hands of the Maxwell family in the mid-thirteenth century where it remained until 1966 when Mrs Anne Maxwell Macdonald gifted Pollok House and its grounds to the city. This view shows the south facade of Pollok House in 1890 with the White Cart river in front of it. While Sir John Maxwell commissioned the house in 1747 it was not completed until 1752, just weeks before his death. Although the exterior of the four-storey house was well-proportioned it was almost austere, as were many Georgian houses. The interior, however, was more exuberant, with ornate plasterwork throughout the principal rooms. It was the fourth Maxwell dwelling on the site, the previous three being castles. The next owner, Sir William Stirling Maxwell, collected most of the superb paintings now on display in the house, the Spanish works being particularly fine.

Right: In 1890 Sir John William Maxwell commissioned Edinburgh architect Robert Rowand Anderson to make additions to the house. Faithfully copying the style of the old, Anderson added two wings (one housed a library), substantial service quarters in the basement and a grand entrance hall that softened the north facade's Georgian austerity. Also added were terraces and garden pavilions. Homes of estate workers were demolished – they spoiled the view from the house – and the families were rehoused in nearby Shawlands. Sir John largely created the gardens and began planting the lime avenue leading to the house's north front. Consisting mainly of trees and shrubs such as magnolias, rhododendrons and azaleas, the gardens are of great horticultural value. Sir John was a founder of the National Trust for Scotland, which since 1998 has managed Pollok House on behalf of the city. Today's view shows that the additions to the house greatly enhanced its appearance.

HARBOUR TUNNEL ROTUNDA

The north and south rotundas used to hide the entrances to the Harbour Tunnel

Left: The rotunda on the south bank of the River Clyde photographed in 1920. Both it and its twin on the north bank hid the entrances to the Harbour Tunnel, running south from Finnieston under the river to Mavisbank Quay in Govan. Until its opening on 15 July 1895, the farthest downstream crossing of the river was Jamaica Bridge. Below the rotundas were 24m (80ft) vertical shafts giving access to three tunnels, two for vehicular traffic and one for pedestrians that shared it with a water main (inset). Each rotunda had six hydraulically powered hoists, three for up traffic and three for down. A long flight of steps led to the passenger tunnel. Charges were 3d for horse-drawn vehicles, 1d for a man with a wheelbarrow and ½d for pedestrians. Commercially, the tunnel was a failure and it closed in 1907. In 1913 the Corporation leased it and re-opened it as a free service.

Above: In 1926 the city took control of the tunnel for a payment of £100,000. As time passed, however, the cost of running it became more than the revenue it produced and in 1943 it was closed to vehicles and the lift machinery was removed for scrap. The passenger tunnel was retained, but as the general area became run-down its use declined from 1,500 pedestrians daily in the mid-1950s to around 200 when it closed on 4 April 1980. It's now only used for accessing the water mains. In 1986 the vehicular tunnels were filled in. For a while the rotundas were forgotten about until the north one (far right) was redeveloped during the 1988 Garden Festival as an ice-cream parlour. It reopened as a Dome of Discovery during the 1999 City of Culture celebrations but is now run-down. The south rotunda presently houses a Japanese Restaurant. Both rotundas are B-listed.

QUEEN'S DOCK AND PRINCE'S DOCK

Now home to exhibition centres, media corporations and a state-of-the-art cinema

Left: An aerial view of Queen's Dock and Prince's Dock taken in 1966. Queen's Dock named after Queen Victoria, is on the nearside of the river. When it opened in 1877 at Stobcross on the north bank of the river it had 3km (10,000ft) of quay, two basins and a hydraulic-powered swing-bridge. It provided accommodation for both passenger and cargo ships sailing worldwide. Across the river from the Finnieston Crane, which was completed in 1931 and described as the new electric crane, is Prince's Dock. Originally known as Cessnock Dock, Prince's Dock opened in 1897. Named after Prince George, Duke of York, it had three basins and a canting (turning) basin. Among the companies using the dock in the inter-war years was the Donaldson Line whose *Athenia* was the first British ship sunk after the outbreak of the Second World War – seven hours after the official declaration on 3 September 1939. A U-boat torpedoed her off the Irish coast with the loss of 112 lives.

Above: Although the previous view shows both docks lined with ships they were in decline and in 1969 Queen's Dock closed. Prince's Dock remained active until the 1970s when, except for the canting basin, it was infilled and in 1988 became the site of the Glasgow Garden Festival. Today, except for the Finnieston Crane and the Harbour Tunnel rotundas, the docks are unrecognisable. Occupying the site of Queen's Dock is the Scottish Exhibition and Conference Centre of 1985 and the iconic Clyde Auditorium of 1997, nicknamed the Armadillo because of its aluminium cladding and shape. Prince's Dock houses the Science Centre of 2005, which contains three buildings – the crescent-shaped Science Mall, the IMAX Theatre, which looks like a squat metallic ball, and the Millenium or Glasgow Tower. Left of IMAX is the BBC's headquarters with STV's on its left beside the rotunda. Bottom left is the Clyde Arc or Squinty Bridge as it's been dubbed, opened in 2006.

BROOMIELAW DOCKS

The opening of a subway and the introduction of electric trams proved disastrous for the Clyde steamers

Left: This scene of 1895 shows the Broomielaw from where the Firth of Clyde pleasure steamers sailed until 1927 when they were moved across river to Bridge Wharf. In the steamers' heyday, Glasgow Fair Saturday saw thousands of people leaving for a trip 'doon the watter', Rothesay a favoured destination. Leaving the quay is the *Daniel Adamson*, originally *Chancellor II*. Purchased by Captain William Buchanan in 1884 she sailed from the Broomielaw to Rothesay and the Gareloch. Berthed is the *Benmore*, built in 1876 by Thomas Seath & Co of Rutherglen. She sailed under the Buchanan flag mostly on the Rothesay run. Canting in midstream is *Iona III*, built in 1864 for David Hutcheson & Co., later David MacBrayne. Left, just in the view is one of the waterbuses known as cluthas (after the Gaelic name for the Clyde) that operated on the river for the three miles between Victoria Bridge and Whiteinch Ferry for a penny a time.

Above: Shortly after the 1895 view was taken, the *Daniel Adamson* was scrapped. In 1920 the *Benmore* was badly damaged by fire and in 1923 was scrapped. The *Iona* became the longest-serving Clyde steamer. After 72 years of service she was retired and broken up in March 1936. The last clutha sailed on 30 November 1903. The opening of the subway in 1897 and the introduction of electric trams in 1901 proved disastrous for them. In the 1960s the new trend towards taking foreign package holidays heralded the end of the Clyde steamers. Only one remains, *PS Waverley*, the world's last surviving paddle steamer. Today's view shows a vastly different river. Not a ship or shed in sight.
A casino now sits on the quayside where passengers waited to embark and disembark from the steamers. Downriver is the Tradeston Bridge (nicknamed the Squiggley Bridge) of 2009, built for pedestrians and cyclists. Behind, is the Kingston Bridge of 1989.

INDEX